XERISCAPE PLANT GUIDE

DENVER WATER

INTRODUCTION BY ROB PROCTOR

Denver Water
American Water Works Association
Fulcrum Publishing

USDA Zone Map

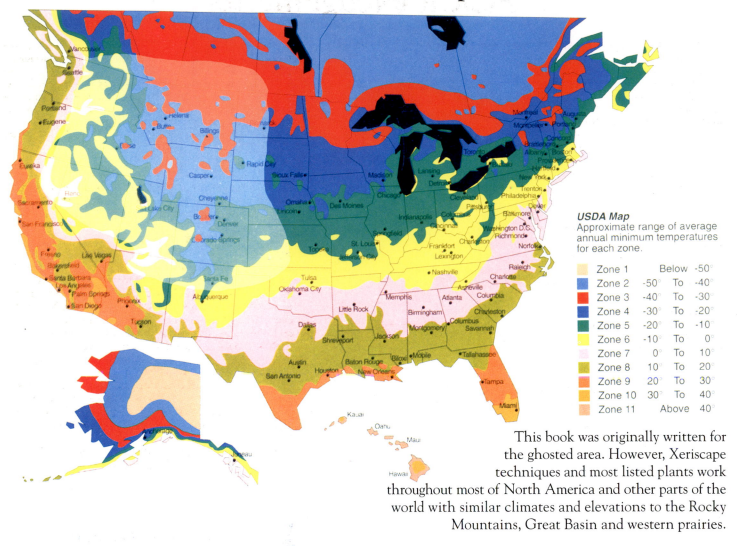

USDA Map
Approximate range of average annual minimum temperatures for each zone.

Zone 1	Below	-50°
Zone 2	-50° To	-40°
Zone 3	-40° To	-30°
Zone 4	-30° To	-20°
Zone 5	-20° To	-10°
Zone 6	-10° To	0°
Zone 7	0° To	10°
Zone 8	10° To	20°
Zone 9	20° To	30°
Zone 10	30° To	40°
Zone 11	Above	40°

This book was originally written for the ghosted area. However, Xeriscape techniques and most listed plants work throughout most of North America and other parts of the world with similar climates and elevations to the Rocky Mountains, Great Basin and western prairies.

Copyright © 1996 Denver Water

Library of Congress Cataloging-in-Publication Data

Proctor, Rob.
    Xeriscape plant guide / introduction by Rob Proctor.
      p.   cm.
    Includes bibliographical references (p. 177) and index.
    ISBN 1-55591-253-2 (paperback)
    ISBN 1-55591-322-9 (hardcover)
    1. Drought tolerant plants—North America. 2. Drought tolerant plants—North America—Pictorial works. 3. Botanical illustration. 4. Xeriscaping—North America. I. Title.
58439.8.P76   1996
635.9'5—dc20
                                  95-52349
                                      CIP

Cover Photograph © 1996 Charles Mann
Cover Illustration © 1996 Angela Overy
Cover and Book Design by Beckie Smith

Printed in China

0 9 8 7 6 5 4

Fulcrum Publishing
16100 Table Mountain Parkway, Suite 300, Golden, Colorado 80403
(800) 992-2908 • (303) 277-1623
www.fulcrum-books.com

Acknowledgements

This book is a cooperative effort by several organizations and individuals, and most of the efforts were volunteer. Members of Xeriscape Colorado provided the overall direction to the Guide plus data from their own research and from their own gardening experience. Photographers from all over the Colorado's Front Range, Western Slope and New Mexico scoured gardens everywhere and their own files for just the right subjects. The Jefferson County Cooperative Extension horticulturist worked diligently to edit initial research. Horticulturists from Denver metropolitan garden centers, garden design businesses and Hudson Gardens, checked and double-checked for accuracy in the text, illustrations and photos. The Denver Botanic Gardens' plant illustration classes formed a special class of volunteer artists to illustrate each plant for close-up identification. The cities of Aurora, Colorado Springs, Castle Rock, Fort Morgan, Grand Junction, Greeley, Longmont, Loveland Water & Power and Platte Canyon Water & Sanitation District provided funds to make *Xeriscape Plant Guide* affordable.

It took three years, thousands of collective hours and dollars to bring this project to fruition. Denver Water and the American Water Works Association are immensely grateful to the following individuals for their hard work and support for *Xeriscape Plant Guide*.

DENVER WATER EDITOR
David Winger

ART DIRECTION & GRAPHIC DESIGN
Beckie Smith

XERISCAPE COLORADO
VOLUNTEER EDITORIAL COMMITTEE
Landscape Architects and Designer:
Ken Ball • Don Godi • Tom Stephens • Marcia Tatroe

XERISCAPE COLORADO PLANT RESEARCH VOLUNTEERS
Professional and non-professional gardeners, landscape contractors, designers, architects and horticulturalists: Maryann Adams • Denise Brady • Jan Caniglia • Sara Delaloye • Connie Ellefson • Mary Ellen Keskimaki • Lisa Manke • Laura Mullen • Kathy Olsen • Donna Pacetti • Connie Rayor • Anne Sturdivant Walz • Marcia Tatroe • Gayle Weinstein • Amy Wright • Jill Ziebell

VOLUNTEER ART INSTRUCTORS AND ARTISTS
Marjorie C. Leggitt • Angela Overy • Rob Proctor

REVISING AND ORGANIZING
Judy Booton • Jane Earle • Pat Gonzales •
Connie McGraw • Leslie Parker • Ethan Saunders

VOLUNTEER HORTICULTURAL REVIEW
Professional Horticulturalists: Robert Cox • Ray Daugherty •
Kelly Grummons • Harriet McMillen • Bob Nold • Andrew Pierce •
Marcia Tatroe • Susan Yetter

VOLUNTEER ARTISTS
Karen Boggs • Jill Buck • Cynthia Cano • Melody Durrett •
Linda Evans • Susan T. Fisher • Barbara Gregg • Pamela Hoffman •
Patty Homs • Sandie Howard • Jayme S. Irvin • Lynn Janicki •
Allyn Jarrett • Libby Kyer • Ann Lowdermilk • Tanya McMurtry •
Diana J. Neadeau/Zimmermann • Nancy Nelson • Shirley Nelson •
Harriet Olds • Marie Orlin • Tana Pittman • Janice Romine •
Susan Rubin • Lori Rhea Swingle • Marilyn Taylor •
Debbie Brown Tejada • Linda Lorraine Wolfe

PHOTOGRAPHERS
Ken Ball • Connie Ellefson • Robert Heapes • Panayoti Kelaidis •
Ed Leland • Charles Mann • Angela Overy • Kathy Olsen •
Rob Proctor • Alan Rollinger • Karelle Scharff • Scott Stephens •
Lori Stover • Randy Tatroe • David Winger/Denver Water.

MARKETING RESEARCH AND ANALYSIS
Steve Boand • Jon L. Farris

THANKS TO THE DENVER BOARD OF WATER COMMISSIONERS
and Denver Water's Manager Hamlet J. Barry, III for their support in the creation of this book. A special thanks to Charles G. Jordan, Denver Water's Public Affairs Director and Elizabeth Gardener, Denver Water's Water Conservation Officer for their commitment and advocacy to and for this book.

The Denver Botanic Gardens are deeply appreciated for having beautiful gardens available for our photographers and illustrators, and a wonderful library for our research. Thanks are extended to the numerous homeowners and businesses who opened up their gardens to us. We are also thankful for access to the Xeriscape Demonstration Gardens located along the Front Range.

Table of Contents

Introduction

by Rob Proctor

A new wave of gardening sweeps through North America. Call it what you will—Xeriscaping, water-smart gardening, environmentally friendly planting—it is based on common sense. Why, as gardeners, should we torture ourselves, growing plants from radically different climates? Why put the effort into growing plants unaccustomed to the extremes of weather we experience? Why squander precious water on exotics that stand a slim chance of survival or that never fulfill their promise?

The answer is simple. Grow plants that thrive in our specific regions. Seek out and plant perennials, annuals, shrubs, trees, and vines that perform well in our soil, that require minimal supplemental irrigation, that can cope with fluctuations in temperature, and that resist disease and pests.

What are these miraculous plants? Turn the pages of this book. You will find a vast array of them ideally suited for gardens of North America. Some of them are instantly recognizable, already considered classics for their excellent garden performance over many decades. Others may not be so familiar. They may be recent introductions from similar climates around the world, or neglected natives that have yet to gain a wide acceptance among the gardening community. That is the purpose behind this book—to present a broad range of exciting plants that merit attention.

Garden Artists

The *Xeriscape Plant Guide* has a unique look. It showcases the works of 31 Colorado artists. They illustrate the beauty of the featured plants.

Botanical illustration is the art of the science of horticulture, with each artist providing a unique rendering that focuses on the personality of the plant. A drawing or painting can capture the essence of a plant in a way that the camera cannot. The artist can condense the seasons, showing buds, flowers, and fruit or seeds at the same moment, or choose to illustrate a single moment in the life of the plant. The artist also conveys a sense of the pleasure of growing it.

Seasonal photographs add another dimension to understanding the featured species. The text provides vital facts in selecting plants suitable for your garden, situating them correctly, and growing the plants successfully. In addition, you will find suggestions for companion plantings or any disadvantages a plant may offer.

A New Approach

The new wave of gardening started with a reexamination of traditional gardening practices. Water has become an increasingly precious commodity throughout North America. Green lawns and water-guzzling ornamental plants seem out of place in a semiarid environment, just as they do in areas where clean water availability has become an issue. No one wants to deprive home owners of a pleasant patch of green for children and pets to play on, or to deny a gardener the pleasure of cultivating a favorite flower. What the new wave advocates, however, is an environmentally friendly approach to all phases of gardening: group plants by their cultural needs, reduce turf areas and plant grasses with lower water requirements, and devote some areas of the home landscape to native and adaptable exotics that come from climates similar to our own.

An exciting facet of this new style of gardening is its distinct character that reflects the beautiful natural landscape. A water-wise garden should appear as full and lovely as any traditional landscape, but it is more in tune with the harmonies of western North America. By incorporating native perennials and shrubs, it celebrates the beauty of our surroundings, rather than replacing them with aesthetic values from another, wetter part of the country. In conjunction with distinctive building materials of our own region—stone, wood, adobe, and brick—our gardens begin to echo the natural landscape.

Some gorgeous native plants seem to embody the spirit of our regional gardens. Indian blanket blazes in the heat and sun of our summers. Brilliant penstemons shine like jewels under blue skies. Butterfly weed is as dazzling as the fluttering insects it attracts. Wine cup shimmers like fine pink satin and the leaves of Bigtooth Maple turn autumnal shades of crimson and gold.

Add a bounty of adaptable plants to the palette, and we can paint garden pictures of distinction and diversity that reflect the sensibilities of their owners. Some pay homage to past gardening traditions in the form of herbaceous borders or cottage gardens. Other western gardens break new ground, endeavoring to interpret the natural landscape in microcosm or depict it in a new way. Just as an artist can draw on the inspiration of the masters or follow his own creative vision, so may a gardener select from several avenues of approach. That, too, defines our western gardens: we see the diversity of our people in the gardens they create. It is our use of our distinguishing palette of plants, grown in an environmentally-conscious manner, that allows us to create wonderful gardens large and small, city or country, even though the styles vary.

Soil Conversation

Get any group of gardeners together, and the conversation inevitably turns to soil. The character and makeup of the soils throughout North America vary. For the West, soil type may be clay or sand, but there is some common ground. Except for isolated pockets, much of the soil is rich in minerals and poor in organic matter. It is generally alkaline.

One of the frustrations of many gardeners is planting traditional plants and watching their dismal performance. These plants that are so successful in other parts of the country do best in organically rich soil. They need regular irrigation to succeed. They evolved where the soil is the product of millions of years of plant decomposition and plentiful rainfall, producing a deep loam. Without major soil amendment, many western soils cannot sustain them. They have trouble delving their roots into clay soil and have difficulty finding enough moisture in fast draining sandy soil. The tiny particles of clay soil pack together tightly with the consequence that oxygen is often unavailable to plants and drainage is poor. An overzealous gardener may easily compound the problem by overwatering. The oxygen-starved, waterlogged roots rot and the plant dies. It is a strange paradox that in our semiarid climate, as many plants are killed by too much water as they are by drought.

On the other hand, native plants and adaptable ones from regions around the world similar to our own evolved to cope with mineral-rich soil with a low content of organic matter. They thrive in clay or sand, and thin, rocky soil, depending upon their ecological niche. They rely on the sky for water and suffer less during periods of high heat and drought. They are equipped to meet the challenges of growing in our climate.

You do not need to fluff and feed. Most of the plants in this book do best in unadulterated native soil or soil that has been slightly amended. Depending on how much your soil has been abused through the years, it may need a little work. Compacted soil should be thoroughly cultivated to improve its tilth. Heavy clay may benefit from the incorporation of organic matter such as compost or well rotted manure. Peat moss is not recommended in that it provides little or no nutritive value and adds to the destruction of the continent's natural resources and ecosystems. Advice about soil improvement from sources outside this region is usually geared toward traditional types of plants

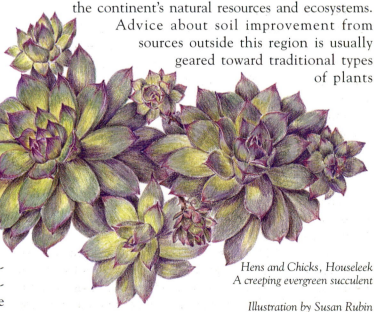

Hens and Chicks, Houseleek
A creeping evergreen succulent

Illustration by Susan Rubin

and often advocates the addition of lime, gypsum, and other materials. This advice should be discounted, no matter what type of plants you wish to grow.

Where topsoil has been ruined or removed by construction, sometimes the only option for a home owner is to start from scratch with store-bought topsoil. This may also be an option in urban areas where soil has been contaminated and compacted by years of parking or dumping. Gardeners in very rocky areas may select this option as well, since it is impossible to create soil where it does not exist.

Few of the plants featured in this book benefit from supplemental irrigation or fertilization since it promotes lush growth in species that are used to a lean and mean regimen. Easy living makes them fat and floppy, leading to an early death. Some of the annuals may perform better with moderate rates of well-balanced fertilizer since their life cycle encompasses only a single season. Newly planted perennials, shrubs and trees require supplemental moisture until they are established. In addition, when extreme conditions of heat and drought prevail over extended periods, even Xeriscape plants can use a helping hand.

No plant, of course, comes with an iron clad guarantee. The best results come from doing your homework. Know the cultural requirements of the plant before you site it. Situate a new plant where it receives the correct amount of light and moisture. Take care in planting so as not to damage roots and set the plant at the same level that it was at in its pot. Water thoroughly; even water-wise plants need to be carefully monitored during their first year. Stick a finger several inches into the soil to determine whether water is necessary. Just touching the surface is not enough.

Some of these featured plants are relatively new to cultivation, and their perameters are just being explored. We become plant pioneers when we experiment with them. Many gardeners prefer to stick with plants that perform reliably in their zone. The United States Department of Agriculture famous map is the basis for these zones (see page ii). Based on average minimum temperatures, it is helpful in making a determination whether a plant will survive a winter in your area.

Hardiness is based on far more than low temperatures. Exposure—whether a plant is exposed to the full force of the wind and sun or has protection from them in the winter—is an important factor in determining hardiness. Drainage and soil type influence hardiness as well. The western plains experience relatively dry winters. That is a bonus since plants do not rot as they often do in a moist climate. On the other hand, snowfall is irregular. Snow protects plants from sun and desiccating winds. A blanket of snow often insulates plants in mountain gardens. This allows gardeners to try many more plants—especially perennials—than their zone assignment might suggest.

Gardening is an adventure. It is up to each of us to explore the options in our own backyard. Planting to take advantage of natural microclimates around our homes affords many opportunities. A sunny, southern exposure might become home to stalwart western wildflowers such as sulphur flower, blue flax, and rabbitbrush, while a bed on the north or east side of a house might provide better wind protection or more reliable snow cover in winter for thyme, lavender or quince. Patterns of sun and shade vary through the seasons and this should be taken into account as well.

Four Seasons of Beauty

Planting and growing water-wise plants might open your eyes. The old garden aesthetic—valuing green grass and tidy rows above all—might become a thing of the past. The new wave of gardening places importance on plants in all four seasons—as they first emerge from the soil, open their blossoms, set seed, and finish their life cycle. It is the appreciation of a plant throughout the year that distinguishes Xeriscape gardening. We value a plant for its flowers and the bees, butterflies and hummingbirds they attract. We appreciate a plant's foliage as it changes throughout the year. We admire its seed heads and the life they bring to the garden, whether it is the promise of seedlings in the spring or the activity of finches and jays that feed on them. Finally, we watch a plant as winter enfolds it. Junipers turn lavender and burgundy while grasses fade from green to gold to tan. Snow dusts pine needles and frost coats the stems of dormant shrubs and perennials.

The cycle is at an end. Winter gives way to spring and the gardener returns to the soil. Old growth is cut away to make room for emerging sprouts. The garden is set for another season in the Rocky Mountain West. The gardener knows that, no matter the course of events of the new season—heat, cold, drought, or wind—the plants will perform beautifully. All of those involved in the making of this book hope your garden of Xeriscape plants will bring you lasting pleasure.

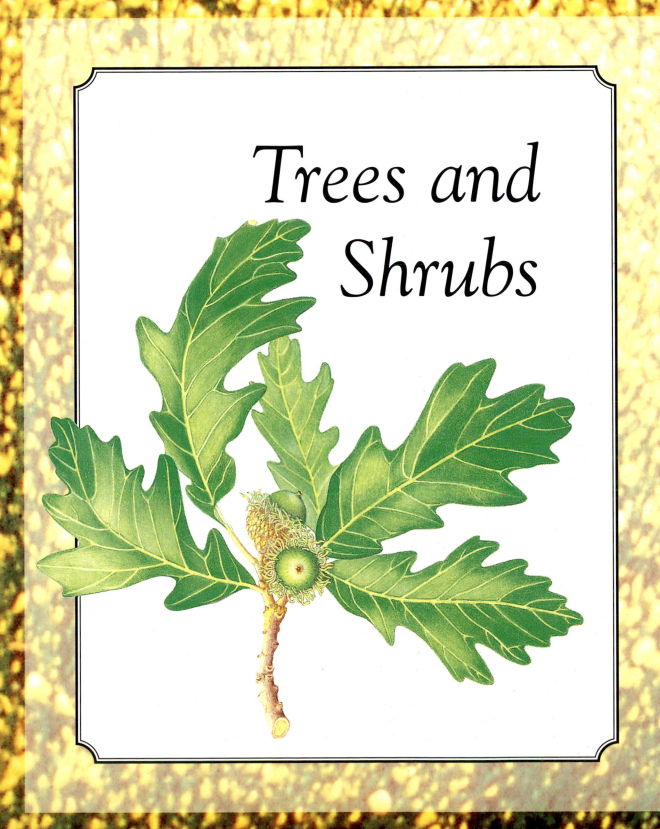

Trees and Shrubs

Acer ginnala

A-ser gi-NA-la
Amur Maple, Ginnala Maple
Aceraceae—Maple Family

Small Tree or Shrub
HEIGHT: 15 to 20 feet
SPREAD: 15 to 20 feet, single or multi-trunked

Illustration by
Cynthia Cano

Late-summer samaras and spring bloom.

*Amur Maple
in spring garden*

LANDSCAPE USE

Excellent specimen tree for small yards or patios, or for grouping, massing or screening. Good small tree under power lines.

FORM

Round to irregular shape. Small tree may be single- or multi-stemmed.

NATIVE RANGE

North China, Mongolia, Manchuria, Korea, Japan. Good to 8,500 feet in Colorado.

CHARACTERISTICS

FLOWER: not particularly showy, yellowish-white, 1/2-inch, forming small panicles. Bloom time is late spring. Fragrant.
LEAVES: medium green, 3- to (rarely) 5-lobed, 3$\frac{1}{2}$ inches long and 2$\frac{1}{2}$ inches wide. Variable fall colors in shades of yellow, orange or red.
FRUIT: 3/4 to 1-inch samaras turn reddish green and are persistent through winter.
TWIGS: often reddish when young. Trunk and branches become "striped" with age.

Spring

CULTURE

SOIL: prefers sandy but adaptable to most soil types. Needs a pH less than 7.5 or may experience chlorosis.
EXPOSURE: full sun but tolerates part shade.
PROPAGATION: softwood cuttings made in early summer. Seed sown in early fall will germinate the next spring.
WATER: low but requires some supplemental watering.
HARDINESS ZONES: 2 to 8.
LIFE SPAN: long, slow growing.

BEST FEATURES

Great fall color, good tree for smaller yard. Very easy to transplant; cold hardy; good tree for mountain gardens.

COMPANION PLANTS

Red fall color contrasts attractively with silver tones of *Ceratoides lanata* (Winter Fat) while reflecting red hips of *Rosa glauca* (Redleaf Rose)

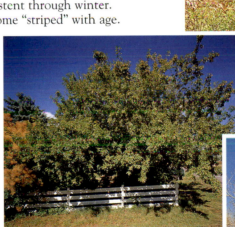
 Summer

DISADVANTAGES

Chlorosis if soil is alkaline. Suckers at base. Occasionally injured by bacterial blights or insects common to maples. Does not do well in heavy clay soils. Brittle.

CULTIVARS

A. ginnala 'Durand Dwarf' grows to 3 feet and is useful as hedge. *A. ginnala* 'Compacta' is dense with compact foliage and is slightly reduced in size. *A. ginnala* 'Flame' has samaras that turn bright red in summer; leaves are fiery red in fall. It is superior as a small tree if trained. *A. ginnala* 'Embers' has samaras that are bright red and has outstanding fall color.

OTHER SPECIES

A. tataricum (Tatarian Maple) is similar in size and appearance. Less sensitive to alkaline soil. Red samaras and yellow fall foliage color.

Winter

Fall

3

Acer grandidentatum

A-ser gran-di-den-TA-tum
Bigtooth Maple, Wasatch Maple, Rocky Mountain Sugar Maple
Aceraceae—Maple Family

Deciduous Tree
HEIGHT: 20 to 30 feet
SPREAD: 20 to 30 feet

Illustration by
Cynthia Cano

Summer and fall leaves with samaras.

LANDSCAPE USE
Small specimen tree, large shrub for screening.

FORM
Usually multi-stemmed, broad, rounded with upright rigid branches.

NATIVE RANGE
Canyons and slopes in western Montana, Idaho and Utah, south into Arizona, Texas and northern Mexico. Can survive up to 8,000 feet in Colorado.

CHARACTERISTICS
FLOWER: greenish yellow in early spring although not particularly showy.
LEAVES: dark green, 5-lobed leaves with large blunt teeth. Range of fall colors are from yellows through reds and burgundy. Fall color is determined by genetic variability (indicating the wisdom of making a fall purchase to check the color). Plant in the spring for best survival potential.
FRUIT: rose-tinted samaras form in late summer.
BARK: smooth and gray.
ROOT: shallow.

CULTURE
SOIL: adaptable to sand through clay as long as it is well drained.
EXPOSURE: sun or preferably light shade.
PROPAGATION: seeds or grafting. Young nursery stock is often wispy and unappealing, belying its future attractiveness.
WATER: moderate to dry; best with occasional deep soaking.
TOLERATES: pruning to form a central leader or to thin out shaded interior branches; slightly acid soil and hot locations.
HARDINESS ZONES: 3 to 8.
LIFE SPAN: long.

BEST FEATURES
Individuals with red fall color are stunning in the landscape.

COMPANION PLANTS
Mahonia repens (Creeping Grape Holly) and *Berberis thunbergii* 'Crimson Pygmy' (Barberry 'Crimson Pygmy').

DISADVANTAGES
Bark on young trees is subject to winter sunscald.

CULTIVARS
Some cultivars have been developed by budding the native plant to the rootstock of sugar maple. (These tend not to be cold hardy in zones 5 and below.)

Big-tooth Maple in summer garden

Early-spring flower

◀▼ *Fall*

Winter

Aesculus glabra

ES-koo-lus GLA-bra
Ohio Buckeye, Fetid Buckeye
Hippocastanaceae—Horsechestnut Family

❖

Deciduous Tree
HEIGHT: 25 to 35 feet
SPREAD: 15 to 25 feet

Illustrations by
Cynthia Cano

Fruiting capsule

*Palmately compound leaf,
characteristic of the horsechestnut
family*

*One of several fall leaf colors
that can develop*

LANDSCAPE USE
Shade, specimen, screen, windbreak; excellent for a small yard.

FORM
Strong, ascending branches form a dense, rounded to broad oval tree. Coarse textured in the landscape.

NATIVE RANGE
Midwestern states, chiefly the valleys of the Ohio and Mississippi rivers. Good up to 6,000 feet in Colorado.

CHARACTERISTICS
FLOWER: showy, trumpetlike, creamy yellow flowers about 1 inch long appear as branched, upright clusters of 4 to 6 inches during late spring.

LEAVES: green, paired, opposite on the stem, compound with 5 leaflets arranged as the fingers of a hand. Leaflets are 3 to 5 inches long, oval, sharply tapered at both ends and finely toothed. Fall color is attractive yellow to orange-red and varies among individuals and sometimes from year to year.

FRUIT: reddish tan-colored fruiting capsules are 1 to 2 inches in diameter, prickly, with 1 to 2 poisonous seeds within, which look like a "buck's eye."

BARK: gray with many furrows broken into scaly plates, sour scented.

CULTURE
SOIL: prefers rich loamy soil, but will adapt to any with good drainage. Tolerates slightly alkaline soils.

EXPOSURE: full sun to filtered shade.

PROPAGATION: seed.

WATER: in nature, found in moist locations but will do well once established, with occasional deep watering in the driest summer months.

HARDINESS ZONES: 5 to 7.

LIFE SPAN: moderate.

BEST FEATURES
Attractive foliage and spring flowers. Dense shade. Small size. Minimal disease and insect problems.

COMPANION PLANTS
Ptelea trifoliata (Wafer Ash) and *Rubus deliciosus* (Boulder Raspberry).

DISADVANTAGES
Fruit cleanup. If stressed, the leaves tend to scorch in late summer.

RELATED SPECIES
Aesculus hippocastanum (Common Horsechestnut)—40 to 50 feet tall, large leaves, white flowers. European origin. Suitable only for large areas.

Ohio Buckeye in late-spring landscape

◀ *Summer*

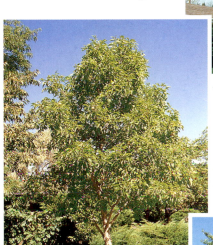

Fall

Winter

Amelanchier alnifolia

am-e-LANG-ki-er al-ni-FO-li-a
Saskatoon Serviceberry, Rocky Mountain Serviceberry, Western Serviceberry
Rosaceae—Rose Family

❖

Multi-stemmed Shrub or Small Tree
Height: 10 to 12 feet
Spread: 20 feet

Illustration by
Marilyn Taylor

Spring flowers transform to purple edible berries by midsummer.

LANDSCAPE USE
Use as a specimen plant, hedge, in shrub or mixed border; fits nicely in a naturalistic setting. Attractive to wildlife.

FORM
Upright, arching branches forming a rounded crown.

NATIVE RANGE
Found at the 5,000- to 10,000-foot elevations of the Rocky Mountain states and at the higher latitudes of the Great Plains to Michigan, north into Manitoba and the Yukon. Adaptable to stream banks, moist meadows and to dry mountain slopes.

CHARACTERISTICS
FLOWER: clusters of simple, fragrant, white flowers appear at the time the leaves emerge in early spring.

LEAVES: emerging leaves change from a medium green to a dark green by summer and to a yellow or soft red in the fall. Foliage is browsed by deer, elk and moose.

FRUIT: the small, edible, blueberrylike berries ripen sweet and juicy by midsummer. Plains Indians mixed serviceberries, buffalo meat and fat to make pemmican. Very attractive to birds.

BARK: smooth, gray.

ROOT: deep and fibrous.

CULTURE
SOIL: prefers rocky, well drained soils and tolerates alkaline clay soils.

EXPOSURE: full sun to partial shade.

PROPAGATION: seed in the fall; root cuttings in early summer; plant division.

WATER: low water, but may require watering during dry spells.

HARDINESS ZONES: 4 to 5.

LIFE SPAN: long.

BEST FEATURES
Spectacular fall color and showy spring flower. The edible fruit makes good jams and jellies and is attractive to wildlife.

COMPANION PLANTS
In naturalistic settings, serviceberry can be paired with *Quercus gambelii* (Gambel Oak) and *Prunus virginiana* (Chokecherry). Attractive with *Artemisia* or other plants with silver foliage.

DISADVANTAGES
Subject to powdery mildew, leaf miners, borers, pear "slugs" and pear leaf blister mites; not particularly tolerant of pollution. Suckers readily.

CULTIVARS
'Regent' has beautiful foliage, much fruit and a compact form. For abundant fruit, 'Success' is a good choice. There are a number of other species and hybrids that are not as drought tolerant.

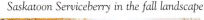
Saskatoon Serviceberry in the fall landscape

Spring

◄ *Summer*

Winter

Fall

Amorpha canescens

ah-MOR-pha can-ES-cens
Leadplant
Fabaceae—Pea Family

Deciduous Shrub
HEIGHT: 1 to 4 feet
SPREAD: 3 to 4 feet

Illustration by
Marilyn Taylor

"Canesens" means gray, fuzzy leaves.

10

Leadplant in midsummer garden

Midsummer

LANDSCAPE USE
A good hardy shrub for sunny locations and well drained soils.

FORM
Erect, slightly arching stems with an open, spreading habit. Fernlike.

NATIVE RANGE
Primarily the Great Plains at the 3,500- to 4,500-foot elevations in Colorado.

Late summer flower

CHARACTERISTICS
FLOWER: long branched, blue or violet spikes at the ends of each stem. Flower season is mid to late summer. Flowers turn yellowish in the fall.
LEAVES: loosely arranged. Made up of small, oval, gray-green leaflets covered with downy white hairs.
FRUIT: 1/4-inch, attractive, sticky pods.
ROOT: deep tap root.

CULTURE
SOIL: dry, well drained or unamended clay.
EXPOSURE: sun.
PROPAGATION: sow seeds in the fall or in the spring, after soaking seed 6 to 8 hours in hot water, follow with cold stratifying for one month. Cuttings are also effective.
WATER: tolerates dry soil better than most shrubs.
HARDINESS ZONES: 5 to 6.
LIFE SPAN: medium.

◄ *Fall*

BEST FEATURES
Does not die back during winter, palatable to wildlife. Nitrogen fixing. Tolerant of air pollution.

COMPANION PLANTS
Calendula officinalis (Pot Marigold) and *Mirabilis multiflora* (Desert Four-o-clock).

DISADVANTAGES
Heavily grazed by cattle and deer. Invasive (suckers) in sandy soil.

RELATED SPECIES
A. fruticosa (False Indigo)—6 to 8 feet tall. *A. nana* (Dwarf Leadplant)—green leaves, pink flowers, 2 feet tall.

Winter

Atriplex canescens

AH-tree-pleks cah-NES-senz
Fourwing Saltbush, Chamiso
Chenopodiaceae—Goosefoot Family

❖

Semievergreen Shrub
HEIGHT: 1 to 6 feet
SPREAD: 4 to 8 feet

Papery bract surrounding seed

Illustration by
Lori Rhea Swingle

Four-winged bracts on stems and leaves are salty to the taste

12

LANDSCAPE USE

Tall ground cover, low hedge or screen, dry parkway or road median, barrier. Good background for intense flower colors. Red sandstone and red or brown brick combined with this plant is very attractive.

FORM

Stout stems, densely branched, forming a rounded spreading mound.

NATIVE RANGE

Grasslands, shrub lands and plateaus at 4,500- to 7,000-foot elevations in Colorado. Occurs in New Mexico, north to South Dakota, west to California from sea level to 8,000 feet.

Four-wing Saltbush in fall garden

CHARACTERISTICS

FLOWER: 4-winged bract, 1/8 to 1/3 inch long, clustered along stems on female plants and form in the spring. Dioecious, with separate male and female plants. Insignificant flower.
LEAVES: tiny, mostly evergreen, linear, silver-green to blue-green, 1/2 inch long, 1/4 to 1/8 inch wide.
FRUIT: showy, papery husk, varying in color from light sulfur yellow, tan to brown.

CULTURE

SOIL: tolerates saline and alkaline soil, very dry soil, intermittently moist and infertile soil and a wide range of soil types. (Do not fertilize.)
EXPOSURE: full sun. Tolerates very harsh, extreme conditions, shelters nearby plants.
PROPAGATION: sow seeds in the fall or early spring.
WATER: very low. Water sparingly for one season, then do not water. Gets by on 6 to 12 inches of water per year.
HARDINESS ZONES: 2 to 10.
LIFE SPAN: long, extremely durable, rapid growth with optimum soil moisture, otherwise moderate.

Spring flower

BEST FEATURES

Extremely tolerant of all conditions.
Very low maintenance. Dried fruit attractive in flower arrangements.

Late-summer seed clusters

COMPANION PLANTS

Combine with dramatic forms of Yucca, Broom, *Ephedra*. Also combine with the dark green foliage of Piñon Pine, Cliffrose or Juniper and with orange, red or yellow flowers.

 Fall

DISADVANTAGES

Not compatible aesthetically or culturally with formal plantings. Best used in "native" settings.

RELATED SPECIES

A. *gardneri* (Saltbush)—white or silver wooly leaf; rigid, dense stems; no conspicuous bracts, inconspicuous flower, 1 to 3 feet high. A. *confertifolia* (Shadscale)— oval leaf, spiny spikes of heart-shaped seeds, 1 to 3 feet high, 4,500- to 7,500-foot elevations.

Winter

Caryopteris x clandonensis

ka-ri-OP-ter-is clan-do-NEN-sis
Blue Mist Spirea
Verbenaceae—Verbena Family

❖

Deciduous Shrub
HEIGHT: 2 to 3 feet
SPREAD: 3 feet

Illustrations by
Diana Neadeau Zimmermann

Flowers profusely in late summer,
decreasing until first frost

Blue Mist Spirea in late summer garden

LANDSCAPE USE
May be used as a shrub or perennial in mixed borders. Best flower display when cut back to about 12 inches in early spring each season. Best appearance when several are massed together or used with other plants.

FORM
Loosely rounded, erect with a soft appearance.

NATIVE RANGE
Asia. Good to 8,500 feet in Colorado.

CHARACTERISTICS
FLOWER: blue flowers in profuse clusters in late summer.
LEAVES: arrowhead-shaped, soft grayish green.
STEMS: stiff and upright.

CULTURE
SOIL: average garden soil that is well drained and neutral to alkaline.
EXPOSURE: full sun.
PROPAGATION: stem cuttings, division and seed.
WATER: requires an occasional deep soaking, but is generally adaptable to dry conditions.
HARDINESS ZONES: 5 to 10.

Late summer

Early summer

BEST FEATURES
Outstanding for late summer color followed by seed heads that are appealing all winter. Attracts butterflies.

COMPANION PLANTS
Chamaebatiaria millefolium (Fernbush) and *Helianthus maximiliani* (Maximilian Sunflower)

DISADVANTAGES
Can be killed by very hard winters; don't cut back until spring, very attractive to bees. Dead head to prevent reseeding.

◄Fall

CULTIVARS
'Azure'—bright blue flowers; 'Blue Mist'—lighter blue flowers; 'Dark Knight'—deep blue purple flowers; 'Longwood Blue'—lavender-blue, gray-green foliage, compact habit; 'Worchester Gold'—golden foliage with blue flowers.

Winter

15

Catalpa speciosa

ka-TAL-pa spee-see-OH-sa
Western Catalpa, Northern Catalpa
Bignoniaceae—Trumpet Creeper Family

Deciduous Tree
HEIGHT: 40 to 70 feet
SPREAD: 20 to 40 feet

A stately tree enhanced by showy summer flowers and seedpods, which provide winter interest

Illustration by
Ann Lowdermilk

LANDSCAPE USE
Specimen, shade; parks, street.

FORM
Large, upright branches form an irregular, open crown. Coarse textured, summer and winter.

NATIVE RANGE
Southern Illinois to Arkansas. Good to 6,000 feet in Colorado.

CHARACTERISTICS
FLOWER: large, white with some purplish streaks, fragrant, 2-inch diameter; trumpet-shaped flowers emerge to cover the tree in early summer.
LEAVES: large, medium green, whorled or opposite on the stem, tropical looking, heart-shaped, (6 to 10 inches). Not a particularly showy yellow in the fall.
FRUIT: 10 to 15 inches long; brown bean-shaped seed capsules form in midsummer and persist into the winter.
BARK: gray-brown with deep furrows.

CULTURE
SOIL: adaptable to almost any soil.
EXPOSURE: sun.
PROPAGATION: seed, root cuttings. Young nursery trees will generally *not* have a large, attractive crown, but will mature quickly.
WATER: low to moderate; benefits from deep watering during prolonged drought.
HARDINESS ZONES: 4 to 8.
LIFE SPAN: medium, moderate to fast growing.

BEST FEATURES
Grows easily in difficult areas. Unusually well adapted to extremes of heat and cold. Provides dense shade. Fast growing, but has strong limbs. Delightfully fragrant flowers. Often grown just for great fenceposts in the Midwest.

COMPANION PLANTS
Chamaebatiaria millefolium (Fernbush) and *Shepherdia argentea* (Buffaloberry).

DISADVANTAGES
Large leaves may suffer hail and wind damage. Messy, fallen flowers in summer, seed capsules and leaves in fall; but the debris is large and coarse, so cleanup is easier than with some trees.

RELATED SPECIES
Chilopsis linearis (Desert Willow)—shorter southwestern relative but with similar showy flowers; marginally hardy in Denver area. *Catapa ovata* (Chinese Catalpa) — similar in leaf, but with creamier flowers. Possibly hardier, generally smaller plant.

Catalpa in early fall garden

Early summer

◄ *Midsummer*

Fall

Winter

Celtis occidentalis

SELL-tis ok-si-den-TA-lis
Common Hackberry
Ulmaceae—Elm Family

Deciduous Tree
HEIGHT: 50 to 60 feet
SPREAD: 40 to 50 feet

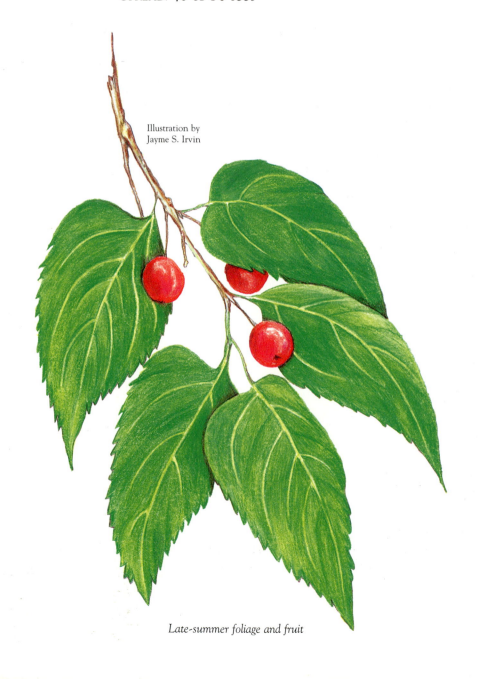

Illustration by
Jayme S. Irvin

Late-summer foliage and fruit

LANDSCAPE USE

Street tree, shade, parking islands, windbreak. Easy to establish on sites where it may be difficult for other trees to grow.

FORM

Upright branches arch to create a high, dense canopy in a broad oval shape.

NATIVE RANGE

Eastern United States from North Dakota to Florida and from northern Texas to southern Maine. Good to an elevation of 7,000 feet in Colorado.

CHARACTERISTICS

FLOWER: inconspicuous clusters.
LEAVES: light, dull green and rough above, slightly paler and fuzzy along the veins below. Turn light yellow in the fall. Long, slightly offset teardrop shape, $2^1/_2$ to 4 inches long $1^1/_2$ to 2 inches wide with finely toothed edges. Alternately spaced on the stem.
FRUIT: fleshy, orange-red; drupe ripens to deep purple in the fall.
BARK: thick, light gray to dark brown, with distinctive knobby ridges.
ROOT SYSTEM: deep and widespread, making it drought resistant.

CULTURE

SOIL: adaptable to a wide range of soil types, tolerating compaction, salt, acidity and alkalinity.
EXPOSURE: full sun and light shade.
PROPAGATION: seed; best if purchased from nursery.
TOLERATES: urban air pollution, wind and late spring snowstorms.
WATER: adaptable to a wide range of soil moisture from moist to dry. Once established, needs little supplemental water.
HARDINESS ZONES: 4 to 9.
LIFE SPAN: moderate; fairly rapid growth rate.

BEST FEATURE

Adaptable to a variety of sites. Attractive, dense canopy.

COMPANION PLANTS

Shade-loving plants such as *Arctostaphylos uva-ursi* (Kinnikinnick) or *Bergenia cordifolia* (Heartleaf Bergenia).

DISADVANTAGES

Extremely prone to get Hackberry nipplegall on the leaves. The psyllid insect that causes this is ubiquitous on Hackberry. Other than an annoyance, it does no harm to the tree.

OTHER CULTIVARS AND SPECIES

'Prairie Pride'—improved leaf and structure. *C. reticulata* (Netleaf Hackberry)—a shrub or small tree (20 to 25 feet) native to the southwestern United States; very drought hardy.

Hackberry in late summer landscape

▲*Young Hackberry in spring landscape*

◀*Fall*   *Winter*

Ceratoides lanata

(formerly *Eurotia lanata*)
cer-a-TOY-deez or you-RO-sha la-NA-ta
Winterfat, White Sage
Chenopodiaceae—Goosefoot Family

❖

Perennial Subshrub
HEIGHT: 1 to 3 feet
SPREAD: 2 to 4 feet

Illustration by
Tana Pittman

The name, "Winterfat," pertains to its excellent forage quality for livestock and wildlife during the winter.

LANDSCAPE USE
Foreground to deep green foliage plants, naturalized areas mixed with grasses or as a background to colorful ground covers.

FORM
Open, upright or bending, herbaceous stems arising from a woody base.

NATIVE RANGE
From southern Canada to northern Mexico and throughout the arid western United States. Found near sea level in Death Valley to over 10,000 feet in the mountains of central Utah.

CHARACTERISTICS
FLOWER: bluish green flowers and bracts appear in the spring along most of the stem.

LEAVES: small, narrow, pale blue green. Leaves, herbaceous stems and flowers are covered with woolly hairs, white early in the spring then turning to a pale rust as the plant matures.

FRUIT: seed heads become cottony and very attractive as they ripen.

CULTURE
SOIL: grows in a wide variety of soil textures including clay, sandy and rocky. Does well in alkaline soil.

EXPOSURE: full sun.

PROPAGATION: sow seed in spring.

TOLERATES: heat, cold and drought.

WATER: low to high. Native conditions range from an annual precipitation of 4 to 40 inches.

HARDINESS ZONES: 3 to 7.

LIFE SPAN: long.

BEST FEATURES
Good selection for sites where only the most hardy of plants can survive. Eye-catching contrast to other garden colors and textures. Attractive in cut or dried arrangements. Looks like a "woolly sagebrush."

COMPANION PLANTS
Festuca ovina glauca (Blue Fescue), *Orzyopsis hymenoides* (Indian Rice Grass) and *Callirhoe involucrata* (Poppy Mallow).

DISADVANTAGES
Can take up a fair amount of space in a small landscape.

Early summer

◄ Late summer

Winterfat in its native setting

Cercocarpus ledifolius

sir-ko-CAR-pus lead-i-FO-lee-us
Curl-leaf Mountain-Mahogany
Rosaceae—Rose Family

Broadleaf Evergreen Shrub or Small Tree
HEIGHT: 4 to 15 feet
SPREAD: 4 to 8 feet

Illustration by
Diana Neadeau Zimmermann

*Midsummer seed
with curled leaf and stem*

LANDSCAPE USE

Attractive as a focal interest, particularly as an evergreen in the winter landscape. Also appropriate as a low-water foundation plant or planted in mass on steep banks, in parkways or as an informal hedge. Good evergreen for small yards or spaces. Can be espaliered.

FORM

Erect, irregular, loosely vase-shaped and densely branched to the ground. Also grown as a single-stem tree or multi-stem clump tree. Can be pruned into a hedge.

NATIVE RANGE

Western North American mountain slopes at 3,000 feet to 9,000 feet in Arizona, California, Utah and Idaho.

CHARACTERISTICS

FLOWER: small, yellowish flowers appear briefly in early spring.
LEAVES: leathery, lustrous, dark green above, white fuzzy below, narrow, 1/2 to 1 inch long.
FRUIT: seeds with white feathery 2- to 3-inch-long taillike plumes.
BARK: light gray, almost white, especially in branch tips.

CULTURE

SOIL: gravelly, rocky, shallow, warm and well drained.
EXPOSURE: full sun or half-day shade.
PROPAGATION: seeds have 50 to 70 percent germination rate. Sow seeds in the fall. Plant nursery stock in the spring for best root development and to prevent winter leaf scorch.
TOLERATES: pruning, even heavy pruning.
WATER: low. Water to establish, then can go unirrigated except in hot dry weather.
HARDINESS ZONES: 3 to 8.
LIFE SPAN: very long lived, slow growing, about at the rate of pines.

BEST FEATURES

Dense, lustrous, evergreen foliage, white, stout branches, feathery white plumes. Little or no maintenance.

COMPANION PLANTS

Quercus gambelii (Gambel Oak) and *Quercus turbinella* (Blue Holly-Leaf Oak). Use with silver foliage plants, sages and winter grasses. *Arctostaphylos*, *Yucca* and *Oenothera* spp.

DISADVANTAGES

Slow growth demands patience.

RELATED SPECIES

Cercocarpus montanus (True Mountain-Mahogany)—deciduous, 6 to 20 feet; with a light green, wedge-shaped, leathery leaf, russet in the fall. 4,000- to 8,500-foot elevations in Colorado. *Cercocarpus intricatus* (Dwarf Mountain-Mahogany)—very dense, rounded form, under 4 feet tall, fine texture with tiny, almost needlelike leaves; 4,500- to 8,500-foot elevations in Colorado.

Curl-leaf Mountain Mahogany in summer garden.

◄ *Spring flower*

Summer

◄ *Fall*

Winter

Chamaebatiaria millefolium

kam-ee-bah-tee-AR-ia mil-le-FOL-e-um
Fernbush
Rosaceae—Rose Family

❖

Semi-evergreen Shrub
HEIGHT: 4 to 6 feet
SPREAD: 4 to 6 feet

Illustrations by
Susan T. Fisher

Midsummer flower spike

*Fernlike foliage that remains
most of the year*

LANDSCAPE USE
Midsummer accent, unshorn hedge, screen, planted in mass.

FORM
Upright, fuzzy stems splay out from the center forming a rounded or somewhat irregular habit.

NATIVE RANGE
Over most of the western states in semiarid locations. Can be established up to 7,000 feet in Colorado.

CHARACTERISTICS
FLOWER: white blossoms resembling those of strawberries are clustered on upright panicles, covering the plant in mid to late summer. Trim off dead flowers to improve appearance.

LEAVES: foliage is aromatic, fernlike (resembles garden tansy), fuzzy and sticky, somewhat leathery and remains green most of the year, finally falling off during early winter and reappearing in late winter in cold climates. In warmer climates leaves remain year-round.

BARK: shreddy, reddish.

CULTURE
SOIL: most any well drained soil.

EXPOSURE: full sun.

TOLERATES: drought and heat.

PROPAGATION: sow in spring; no stratification necessary, only a little moisture.

WATER: once established requires little supplemental water except in the driest periods.

HARDINESS ZONES: 5 to 10.

LIFE SPAN: long.

BEST FEATURES
Showy, fragrant, summer flowers. Attracts bees and butterflies. Low maintenance. Some gardeners prefer leaving the seedheads on all winter for their interest and then trimming them in the spring.

COMPANION PLANTS
Amorpha canescens (Leadplant) and *Chrysothamnus nauseosus* (Rabbitbrush).

DISADVANTAGES
Attracts bees.

Fernbush in midsummer garden.

◀ *Spring*

Late Summer

◀ *Fall*

Winter

Chrysothamnus nauseosus

cry-so THAM-nus naw-zee-O-sus
Rubber Rabbitbrush,
Gray Rabbitbrush, Chamisa
Asteraceae—Sunflower Family

Deciduous Shrub
HEIGHT: 2 to 6 feet
SPREAD: 2 to 4 feet

Illustration by
Jill Sanders Buck

*"Chamisa" means
yellow-flowered shrub.*

*Rubber Rabbitbrush
in late-summer garden*

Spring

LANDSCAPE USE
Very dry areas; good for traffic islands, south-facing slopes.
Serves well as a background or mixed with the flowers of Purple Aster and Russian Sage, which blossom at about the same time.

FORM
Irregular globe-shaped, multi-stemmed, woody base with herbaceous stems. Young plant is compact. Mature plant is more open. Plant has a soft natural appearance in the landscape.
NATIVE RANGE: 5,000- to 9,000-foot elevations in Colorado. All subspecies are native to the Rocky Mountains from Saskatchewan and British Columbia to New Mexico and Arizona. Natural environment includes the plains, semideserts and mountain plateaus.

◀ *Summer*

CHARACTERISTICS
FLOWER: always yellow, formed in clusters at the tips of new growth. Strongly scented. Bloom time is late summer and early fall.
LEAVES: numerous, slender, blue-green, needlelike.
FRUIT: fluffy seed clusters are persistent throughout the winter and early spring.

CULTURE
SOIL: well drained, alkaline.
EXPOSURE: sunny.
TOLERATES: annual early spring pruning to 1-foot height to maintain its globe shape. Provides browse for sheep, deer and rabbits.
PROPAGATION: by seeds; best purchased at a nursery.
HARDINESS ZONES: 4, 5 and 6.
LIFE SPAN: long, fast growing.

Winter

BEST FEATURES
Brilliant flower display that attracts bees and butterflies. Attractive winter form. Uses have included yellow dye, tea and cough medicine. Was once considered as a possible rubber source.

COMPANION PLANTS
Zauschneria spp. (Hummingbird Flower), *Cercocarpus ledifolius* (Curl-leaf Mtn. Mahogany), *Callirhoe involucrata* (Poppy Mallow) and native grasses.

DISADVANTAGES
May reseed readily. Deadheading will prevent reseeding but at the cost of winter interest.

SUBSPECIES
Harrington recognizes 6 subspecies in Colorado with slight differences and notes that each is evolving by cross-pollination. *C. n. albicaulis* is the most commonly found subspecies in the trade.

Fall

27

Cotoneaster divaricatus

ko-TON-ee-a-ster di-vah-ri-Kah-tos
Spreading Cotoneaster
Rosaceae—Rose Family

❖

Deciduous Shrub
HEIGHT: 3 to 5 feet
SPREAD: 6 to 8 feet

Illustration by
Linda Lorraine Wolfe

Berries provide color for three seasons.

LANDSCAPE USE

Use as boundary, informal hedge or screen, large bank planting, foundation planting. They are especially attractive spilling over a wall or rocks.

FORM

Wide spreading with upright, arching stems originating from the center. Stems are trimmed with small leaves.

NATIVE RANGE

China.

CHARACTERISTICS

FLOWER: white to pink in late spring, showy but partially hidden by foliage. Attractive to bees.
LEAVES: 3/4-inch, egg-shaped, shiny and dark green. Leaves grow alternately along the full length of the stems. Orange to red fall color.
FRUIT: 1/3-inch red pomes (berries) form in late summer. Attractive to birds in winter.

CULTURE

SOIL: adapts well to poor soils if carefully planted and tended until established. Prefers neutral to slightly acid and well drained.
EXPOSURE: full sun.
Will tolerate afternoon shade.
PROPAGATION: start from cuttings or layering in early summer. Difficult to transplant large plants.
WATER: low to moderate.
TOLERATES: pruning anytime.
HARDINESS ZONES: 5 to 7.
LIFE SPAN: long, slow growth rate.

BEST FEATURES

Grows vigorously, and thrives with little or no maintenance; great show of berries; tolerant of pollution.

COMPANION PLANTS

Parthenocissus quinquefolia (Virginia Creeper) and *Zauschneria arizonica* (Hummingbird Flower).

DISADVANTAGES

Fire blight (bacterial disease) is possible, but uncommon.

SUBSPECIES OR VARIETIES

None listed for *C. divaricatus*, but there are many other species of Cotoneaster, ranging from ground covers to stiffly upright shrubs, both deciduous and evergreen.

Spreading Cotoneaster in fall garden

Spring flowers

◄ *Summer*

Fall

Winter

29

Cowania mexicana

cow-AN-eea mex-e-CAN-a
Cliffrose, Quinine Bush
Rosaceae—Rose Family

Broadleaf Evergreen Shrub
HEIGHT: 3 to 12 feet
SPREAD: 3 to 6 feet

Illustration by
Melody Durrett

*Flowers appear all summer and are enhanced
by masses of feathery plumes late in the season.*

LANDSCAPE USE

Background for perennials or among perennials because it casts light shade. Excellent as an untrimmed hedge or as a specimen in a dry garden. Ideal for naturalized landscapes. Can be sheared into a hedge.

FORM

Rigid, gnarled branches form an upright, rather open shrub.

NATIVE RANGE

Low hills and canyons of the West, including southwestern Colorado, Utah, Nevada, California, Arizona, New Mexico and Mexico, 4,500- to 7,000-foot elevations in Colorado.

CHARACTERISTICS

FLOWER: light yellow, roselike, fragrant, profusely flowering in early summer and continuing to display a few flowers the rest of the summer.

LEAVES: small, 3-to 5-lobed, wedge-shaped, deep blue-green, alternate.

FRUIT: white, feathery plumes form in mid to late summer, persisting into winter.

BARK: shreddy and light brown.

CULTURE

SOIL: prefers well drained sandy or gravelly but adaptable to any well drained soil.

EXPOSURE: full sun.

TOLERATES: shearing and pruning; however, looks best left natural.

PROPAGATION: seed in the fall.

WATER: low, 10 to 15 inches per year is adequate once it is established. More water causes rampant growth and stress.

HARDINESS ZONES: 4 to 7.

LIFE SPAN: long, moderate growth rate depending upon water availability.

BEST FEATURES

Showy flower display; picturesque irregular form.

COMPANION PLANTS

Achillea filipendulina (Tall Yellow Yarrow) and *Yucca baccata* (Banana Yucca).

DISADVANTAGES

Emits a musky odor (hence "Quinine Bush") that some may find objectionable; good deer and antelope browse.

OTHER SPECIES

Similar in appearance and culture to *Fallugia paradoxa* (Apache Plume) and *Purshia tridentata* (Antelope Bitter Brush), which are lower growing and found primarily on the east slope of the Rockies, while *Cowania* is found on the west slope.

Cliffrose in early-summer garden

◀ *Late-summer seed plumes*

Midsummer

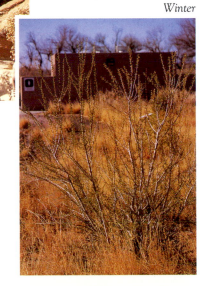

◀ *Fall*

Winter

Crataegus crus-galli

kra-TE-gus krus-GAL-i
Cockspur Hawthorn
Rosaceae—Rose Family

❖

Deciduous Small Tree or Large Shrub
HEIGHT: 20 to 30 feet
SPREAD: 20 to 35 feet

*The species is armed with thorns.
Pictured is var.* inermis *with smooth
thornless stems.*

Illustration by
Allyn Jarrett

LANDSCAPE USE
Specimen plant, informal groupings or as screens, hedges or barriers.

FORM
Round top with unique horizontal branching often growing low to the ground. Distinct habit makes it easy to identify.

NATIVE RANGE
Quebec to Ontario, Illinois and Georgia. The variety *inermis* was first selected at Secrest Arboretum in Wooster, Ohio.

CHARACTERISTICS
FLOWER: white flowers bloom in 2- to 3-inch clusters or flattopped corymbs; have an almond scent, which some have found disagreeable. Flowers appear in late spring and are at their best for 7 to 10 days.
LEAVES: 3 inches, serrated and glossy green, turning bronzy red in the fall.
FRUIT: the red fruit (haws) are 1/2 inch in diameter when they mature during early fall and remain through the winter.
BARK: the soft, gray twigs and small branches are attractive in winter.

CULTURE
SOIL: performs well in most soils, including alkaline, but soil must be well drained.
EXPOSURE: full sun.
PROPAGATION: seed, budding on seedlings.
WATER: adaptable to drought.
HARDINESS ZONES: 4 to 8.
LIFE SPAN: moderate and slow growing.

BEST FEATURES
Tolerates city growing conditions; attractive spring flowers; bronze-red fall color and fruit. A good choice for a small, urban street tree.

COMPANION PLANTS
Vinca minor (Periwinkle) and *Heuchera* spp. (Coral Bell).

DISADVANTAGES
Dense foliage can prevent other plants from growing directly under the tree. Susceptible to insects, fire blight, cedar apple rust and several other diseases; may require some spraying. Thorns can be hazardous to those who come in close contact. Not for children's play areas. Fall colors vary from tree to tree.

SUBSPECIES OR VARIETIES
Crataegus crus-galli var. *inermis* is thornless. 'Crusader' ('Cruzam') is a trademarked disease-resistant variety of *C. crus-galli* var. *inermis*. There are hundreds of hawthorn species in North America and several in Europe.

Cockspur Hawthorn in midsummer garden.

Spring

◀ *Summer*

Fall

Winter

33

Fallugia paradoxa

fahl-OO-gi-a par-ra-DOH-xa
Apache Plume
Rosacea—Rose Family

❖

Deciduous Shrub
HEIGHT: 3 to 5 feet
SPREAD: 3 to 5 feet

Illustration by
Nancy Wilbur Nelson

*Spring flowers produce showy
seeds that last most of the summer.*

Apache Plume
in early-summer
garden.

Spring

LANDSCAPE USE
Fine-textured shrub valuable for dry spots in the garden. Also useful for erosion control and wildlife forage. Provides cover for small mammals and ground-dwelling birds. Best used in massings along highways.

FORM
Lacy appearing mound with dense, slender branches.

NATIVE RANGE
3,500 to 8,000 feet from Utah south to Texas. Abundant in the San Luis Valley and the Arkansas Valley near Pueblo, Colorado. Found on rocky slopes and washes.

CHARACTERISTICS
FLOWER: single, white, roselike flowers bloom all summer simultaneously with its fuzzy seed heads. Blooms on new growth.
LEAVES: very small, wedge-shaped and semievergreen.
FRUIT: russet-mauve feathery plumes that resemble feather dusters turning to tan and collecting in lower portions of plant when dispersed.
BARK: whitish, exfoliating.

 ◀ Summer

CULTURE
SOIL: needs well drained soil; won't tolerate poorly drained clay soil; performs poorly when overwatered; won't tolerate wet winter conditions.
EXPOSURE: full sun.
PROPAGATION: sow seeds anytime or start from softwood cuttings.
WATER: very drought tolerant.
TOLERATES: pruning in spring.
HARDINESS ZONES: 3 to 10.
LIFE SPAN: long.

Fall

BEST FEATURES
Ability to thrive in extreme drought.
Color and interest all summer.

COMPANION PLANTS
Yucca glauca (Soapweed) and *Callirhoe involucrata* (Wine Cup).

DISADVANTAGES
Tendency to sucker and can be slow to get established.

SUBSPECIES OR VARIETIES
It is the only species of this genus in North America but it does hybridize with *Purshia tridentata*.

Winter

Forestiera neomexicana

for-es-STEER-a ne-o-MEX-i-KA-na
New Mexican Privet, Adelia, Desert Olive
Oleaceae—Olive Family

Deciduous Shrub
HEIGHT: 12 to 15 feet
SPREAD: 6 to 10 feet

Illustration by
Melody Durrett

Female plant with fruit.

Pruned as a small tree in midsummer garden.

Spring and summer appearance.

LANDSCAPE USE
Attractive informal hedge; excellent sheared hedge; provides good screen when fast results are needed. Wildlife habitat.

FORM
Upright, multi-stemmed, finely twigged branches create a dense, rounded shrub.

NATIVE RANGE
Colorado to California, Texas to Arizona, west central and southwest Colorado in dry valleys at elevations of 4,500 to 7,000 feet.

CHARACTERISTICS
FLOWER: small, somewhat showy in abundance, yellow-green; flowers occurring in clusters on leaf axil in early to mid-spring before leaves appear. The flowers do not have petals. Need both male and female plants to produce "berries."
LEAVES: 1/2 to 1 inch; bright gray-green; narrowly oval. The leaves are opposite, simple with smooth or sometimes slightly serrated edges. They turn golden yellow in the fall.
FRUIT: 1/4 inch x 1/8 inch; blue-black to black drupe; bitter.
STEMS: attractive tan color.

CULTURE
SOIL: adaptable, prefers well drained; found wild on loam, clay, sand and lava-based soils.
EXPOSURE: full sun.
TOLERATES: pruning in spring to control shape.
PROPAGATION: by layers or cuttings. Seeds need to be stratified for 1 month at 40° F.
WATER: drought tolerant, but adaptable to higher moisture levels.
HARDINESS ZONES: 5 to 8.
LIFE SPAN: long.

BEST FEATURES
Shears well to form windbreak or hedge, or can be pruned as small airy specimen tree. Pest and disease resistant. Attracts birds. Attractive bark, best displayed with lower branches pruned out.

COMPANION PLANTS
Juniperus horizontalis, Yucca spp. *Stachys lanata, Cotoneaster* spp.

DISADVANTAGES
Mildew on foliage may be caused by high moisture content in the soil and poor air circulation.

Winter

Fall

Fraxinus pennsylvanica

FRAK-si-nus pen-sil-VA-ni-ka
Green Ash
Oleaceae—Olive Family

❖

Deciduous Tree
HEIGHT: 50 to 60 feet
SPREAD: 30 to 40 feet

Cultivars provide an appealing growth habit and this attractive foliage without the mess associated with numerous seeds.

Illustration by
Melody Durrett

38

LANDSCAPE USE

Street border, specimen, grove or tall screen, summer shade and windbreak.

FORM

When young, rather open and pyramidal; mature are irregular oval or rounded and spreading. Coarse texture in the landscape, especially in winter.

NATIVE RANGE

North from the Canadian prairie provinces down through the Great Plains to the Gulf Coast, east to the Atlantic up to Maine. Western border is the eastern borders of Montana, Wyoming, Colorado and northeastern Texas. In Colorado, can be established between 4,500 to 7,500 feet.

CHARACTERISTICS

FLOWER: inconspicuous.
LEAVES: compound 10 to 12 inches with 3- to 5-inch, lance-shaped leaflets with smooth or slightly serrated edges, bright green on both sides, turning yellow in the fall.
FRUIT: tan, 1- to 2-inch samaras on female trees.
BARK: tan or light gray, longitudinal, shallow furrows with scaly ridges.
ROOT: wide spreading, and tends to grow near the surface in a well watered lawn.

CULTURE

SOIL: adaptable and tolerates acidity and alkalinity, salt, drought and compaction.
EXPOSURE: full sun.
PROPAGATION: sow seed in the fall. Cultivars are budded onto seedlings.
TOLERATES: air pollution, heat and cold. Cold tolerance depends on cultivar origin.
WATER: moist to dry. Cease irrigation in early fall to improve winter hardiness.
HARDINESS ZONES: 4 to 10.
LIFE SPAN: moderately long; fast growing in moist conditions, slower in dry.

BEST FEATURES

Wide range of growing conditions, attractive foliage, relatively fast growing.

COMPANION PLANTS

Understory can be *Symphoricarpos* x *chenaultii* (Chenault Coralberry) or *Mahonia repens* (Creeping Grape Holly).

DISADVANTAGES

Susceptible to leaf curl, ash aphid, brown-headed ash sawfly and scale. Particularly susceptible to lilac or ash borer if drought stressed. Prone to storm damage, requiring preventive removal of weak or crossed branches. Suckers. Self sowing can be a nuisance.

OTHER CULTIVARS

'Marshall'—seedless (male) clone with dark green leaves. 'Summit'—seedless even though it is a female clone; more of a narrow oval growth habit than the species. 'Patmore'—seedless, symmetrically shaped. 'Cimmaron'—seedless (male), twice as tall as wide, rust-red pale color. 'Leprechaun'—new cultivar, much smaller (to 15 feet). 'Bergeson'—seedless, well defined oval crown; tolerates part shade. *F. mandshurica* 'Mancana' is an outstanding replacement for Green Ash.

Green Ash in fall landscape.

◀ *Spring*

Summer

Winter

39

Gymnocladus dioica

jim-NO-klad-us dy-oy-E-ca
Kentucky Coffee Tree
Fabaceae—Pea Family

Deciduous Tree
HEIGHT: 50 to 60 feet
SPREAD: 30 to 40 feet

*Twice pinnately compound leaf
with seedpod from female tree*

Illustration by
Nancy Wilbur Nelson

LANDSCAPE USE
Specimen tree or a street tree.

FORM
Erect, rounded crown. Young trees are narrow and irregularly shaped. Trees broaden with age, having several large, ascending branches and fewer lateral branches.

NATIVE RANGE
Uncommon throughout its range in the eastern and central United States on moist sites. Survives to 8,000 feet in Colorado.

CHARACTERISTICS
FLOWER: greenish white fragrant clusters in the spring. Usually inconspicuous since they come out after leaves have formed.
LEAVES: double pinnately compound, 18 to 24 inches, divided into many leaflets. Pinkish leaves emerge late in spring, mature to bluish green and conclude as golden in the fall.
FRUIT: tough, hard, curved pods 4 to 6 inch long form on female trees only. Seeds are poisonous and rock hard. Pods remain on tree into winter.
BARK: dark gray, scaly and ridged, deeply fissured.

CULTURE
SOIL: well drained. Tolerates alkalinity, salt and drought.
EXPOSURE: full sun or light shade.
PROPAGATION: seeds. Transplants. Disturbed roots tend to sucker.
WATER: moist to establish, can be maintained under dry conditions thereafter.
HARDINESS ZONES: 4 to 9.
LIFE SPAN: long, slow to medium growth rate.

BEST FEATURES
Picturesque silhouette in winter. In the summer, grass grows well underneath the dappled shade. Adaptable to urban conditions and resistant to diseases and insects. Provides little winter shade, making an excellent tree for southern exposures of solar homes.

COMPANION PLANTS
Buchloe dactyloides (Buffalograss) has a chance of surviving under this tree. *Ribes aureum* (Golden Currant) and *Rosa glauca* 'Rubrifolia' (Red Leaf Shrub Rose) tolerate light shade. *Heuchera* spp. (Coralbells) planted in mass.

DISADVANTAGES
Shed pods can be somewhat messy although not a big problem.

CULTIVARS
None.

Kentucky Coffee Tree in midsummer garden.

◀ *Summer*

Fall

Winter

Hippophae rhamnoides

hip-PO-fay-e ram NOI-deez
Sea Buckthorn
Elaeagnaceae—Oleaster Family

❖

Deciduous Shrub
HEIGHT: 8 to 18 feet
SPREAD: 8 to 12 feet

Branch tip with leaves and thorns.

Female fall berries

Illustrations by
Susan T. Fisher

LANDSCAPE USE
Informal background, barrier plant or hedge, wildlife, naturalizing.

FORM
Erect, thorny shrub.

NATIVE RANGE
Himalayas and China. Can be established up to 7,000 feet in Colorado.

CHARACTERISTICS
FLOWER: small, greenish blossom before leaves emerge, male and female flowers on different plants.
LEAVES: narrow to lancelike, silvery; green on upper side as shrub matures.
FRUIT: orange, firm, berrylike drupes form in late summer on the female plant. Edible.
BARK: brown to gray.

CULTURE
SOIL: adaptable to clay, sandy or gravelly soils. Prefers infertile soil.
EXPOSURE: full sun.
PROPAGATION: seeds, root cuttings or division. Difficult to transplant mature plant.
WATER: dry to moist soils.
TOLERATES: pruning in the spring.
HARDINESS ZONES: 3 to 7.
LIFE SPAN: long due to rhizomatous growth.

BEST FEATURES
Silver foliage, attractive berries through the winter.

COMPANION PLANTS
Combines well with *Shepherdia argentea* (Silver Buffaloberry) and *Perovskia atriplicifolia* (Russian Sage).

DISADVANTAGES
Thorns and suckering habit may be a problem if located in the wrong spot.

Sea Buckthorn in summer garden.

Spring and summer appearance.

◄ *Fall male*

Fall female

Winter

Juniperus horizontalis

june-NIP-er-us hor-i-ZON-ta-lis
Creeping Juniper
Cupressaceae—Cypress Family

Evergreen Shrub
HEIGHT: 6 to 18 inches
SPREAD: 5 to 8 feet

Illustration by
Lori Rhea Swingle

*Creeping Junipers mimimize evapotranspiration with small, densely
packed leaves and a growth habit that shades the soil over the roots.*

'Hughes' Juniper in summer garden.

LANDSCAPE USE
Ground cover, coverage of hillside or bank, cascade over rock wall or in planters.

FORM
Low spreader, usually prostrate, sometimes upright.

NATIVE RANGE
North America, Canada, northern United States from Washington to Maine. Most cultivars do well up to 8,000 feet in Colorado.

CHARACTERISTICS
FLOWER: inconspicuous.
LEAVES: scalelike, overlapping and pressed together, prickly, gray-green, blue-green, green; most varieties are plum-colored in the winter.
FRUIT: small berrylike cones, dark blue. Males produce pollen; females produce cones.
BARK: brown.

◀ *'Blue Chip' Juniper in summer.*

'Wiltoni' Juniper on right side of steps.

CULTURE
SOIL: adaptable to clay, sandy or gravelly soils.
EXPOSURE: prefers full sun, but tolerates some shade.
PROPAGATION: sow seed in the fall.
Cultivars are propagated by cuttings. Best to purchase from nursery.
WATER: dry to moist soil.
HARDINESS ZONES: 3 to 9.
LIFE SPAN: moderate: 20 years.

BEST FEATURES
Evergreen foliage and low growth form.

COMPANION PLANTS
Other evergreens, *Shepherdia* spp. (Buffaloberry), *Yucca* spp. (Yuccas) and many other shrubs.

DISADVANTAGES
As a ground cover, won't tolerate foot traffic.
Often lets weeds or grass grow through.

CULTIVARS
'Bar Harbor'—steel blue foliage, purple winter color, tolerates salt spray. 'Blue Chip'—blue-green foliage, somewhat upright, 10 inches high. 'Hughes'—dense, flat top, good color. 'Wiltoni'—very prostrate, silvery blue foliage, only 4 inches high. Many other cultivars; at least 60 known. Cultivars are male or female.

Plum winter color.

Late-summer cones

Garden

Juniperus scopulorum

ju-NIP-er-us skop-u-LO-rum
Rocky Mountain Juniper
Cupressaceae—Cypress Family

Evergreen Tree or Large Shrub
HEIGHT: to 30 feet in Colorado
SPREAD: 8 to 15 feet

Scalelike leaves

LANDSCAPE USE
Used as screens, hedges, background specimens. Birds use as shelter and eat the fruit.

FORM
Widely variable growth habit but generally pyramidal, often with several main stems.

NATIVE RANGE
Usually above 5,000-foot elevations, and up to 10,000-foot elevations in Colorado. This plant grows on dry rocky slopes all along the Rocky Mountains from Alberta, Canada, to Texas. It is also found as far west as Oregon and Washington.

CHARACTERISTICS
FLOWER: small and simple, not very showy.
LEAVES: are dark or light bluish-green to grayish-green in color with a powdery coating. The leaves are ¹/₄ inch in diameter, scalelike.
FRUIT: berrylike cones that are 1/4 to 1/3 inch in size. They are usually dark blue in color and ripen in the second year. The pulp of the cone has a sweet taste.
BARK: is reddish brown or gray in color and has a shredded texture.

CULTURE
SOIL: well-drained and adaptable to high or low pH.
EXPOSURE: full sun.
PROPAGATION: sow seeds in the fall but easiest to buy seedlings from a nursery.
WATER: is adaptable to dry, clay soils; withstands drought conditions.
HARDINESS ZONES: 3 to 7.
LIFE SPAN: long.
BEST FEATURE: can tolerate a variety of soils and moisture conditions.

Illustration by
Lori Rhea Swingle

COMPANION PLANTS
Looks good with *Mirabilis multiflora* (Wild Four o'clock) or *Juniperus horizontalis* (Creeping Juniper) massed beneath it.

DISADVANTAGES
Branches break easily with heavy, wet snow. The growth rate is very slow. Can be a host plant for the juniper-hawthorn rust disease. Do not plant near crabapples or hawthorns as these plants are alternate hosts for the rust disease.

Branchlet with ripe berrylike cones

CULTIVARS
'Cologreen'—forest green foliage with columnar shape; 'Grey Gleam'—silvery gray foliage and pyramidal in shape; 'Wichita Blue'—silvery blue foliage and a broad, pyramidal shape, plus many others selected for their foliage color or growth habit.

Cytisus scoparius 'Moonlight'

Late-spring landscape

Summer

sigh-TIS-us sco-PAIR-ee-us
Moonlight Broom, Scotch Broom
Fabaceae—Pea Family

Deciduous Shrub
HEIGHT: 4 to 6 feet
SPREAD: 4 to 6 feet

LANDSCAPE USE
Use as a vertical contrast to softer, bushier plants. Plant as a screen or hedge along fences, driveways and paths. Mix with perennials in a border.

FORM
Erect, upright mass of wandlike, bright green stems.

NATIVE RANGE
Spain and Portugal. Good to 7,000 feet in Colorado.

CHARACTERISTICS
FLOWER: 1 inch, creamy yellow pealike flowers appear in late spring and early summer.
Prune after flowering to maintain attractive apperance.
LEAVES: about 1/4 inch long, narrow and bright green.
FRUIT: flat, beanlike pods form. At maturity pods can split noisily, sending seed several feet from the plant.
STEMS: remain green fall through winter.

CULTURE
SOIL: prefers acidic, but tolerates any soil that is well drained, gravelly.
EXPOSURE: full sun.
PROPAGATION: cuttings or occasional layers.
WATER: low, but more attractive with a little summer water.
HARDINESS ZONES: 5 to 10. Extended temperatures below 0° F can cause dieback to the ground. Will resprout from the roots like a perennial the following spring.
LIFE SPAN: long.

BEST FEATURES
Profuse flower display. Will add nitrogen to the soil. Evergreen stems provide winter color.

COMPANION PLANTS
Fallugia paradoxa (Apache Plume) and *Linum perenne* (Blue Flax).

DISADVANTAGES
Transplants poorly, so to maximize success, start with small plants; seeds and pods are toxic when eaten; invasive in warmer zones that do not drop below freezing.
Best to plant in protected location to minimize winter dieback in colder zones.

OTHER CULTIVARS AND SPECIES
'Lena'—2 to 3 feet tall, bright yellow and rust flowers, late-spring bloom. 'Nova Scotia'—bright yellow flowers. C. x *praecox* (Warminster Broom)—compact, 3 to 5 feet tall, bright yellow flowers, mid-spring bloom. Many small relatives are useful in either the flower border or rock garden.

Illustration by
Pamela Hoffman

Almost leafless branches flowering at nodes.

47

Kolkwitzia amabilis

kolk-WITZ-i-a am-AB-ill-is
Beauty Bush
Caprifoliaceae—Honeysuckle Family

❖

Deciduous Shrub
HEIGHT: 6 to 10 feet
SPREAD: 4 to 8 feet

Illustration by
Rob Proctor

Early-summer flower display lasts about two weeks.

Beauty Bush in early-summer garden.

Summer

LANDSCAPE USE
Best in a shrub border rather than used as a specimen plant. Plant near enough to a walk that the early summer flower show can be appreciated.

FORM
Finely branched, multiple upright stems grow outward to form a dense shrub with a broad, rounded habit.

NATIVE RANGE
Central China. Good to 7,500 feet in Colorado.

CHARACTERISTICS
FLOWER: bell-shaped, bright pink flowers with yellow throats in great profusion in early summer.
LEAVES: dark green, oval, 1 1/2 inches long.
FRUIT: bristly, brown capsules provide seasonal interest.
BARK: grayish brown, peeling on lower branches and trunks at maturity.

CULTURE
SOIL: tolerates a wide range of soils.
EXPOSURE: best in full sun but will tolerate partial shade.
PROPAGATION: easy to transplant. Start from softwood cuttings or seed sown in spring.
WATER: moderate drought tolerance, best with occasional deep soaking.
TOLERATES: annual pruning of old stems, which reduces the twiggy appearance.
HARDINESS ZONES: 5 to 8.
LIFE SPAN: long.

BEST FEATURES
Flowers are a show stopper in early summer.

COMPANION PLANTS
Syringa vulgaris (Common Purple Lilac), *Juniperus horizontalis* (Creeping Junipers) and flowering perennials.

DISADVANTAGES
Rather coarse when not in bloom.

CULTIVARS
K. amabilis is the only species in this genus, but two outstanding cultivars are 'Pink Cloud' and 'Rosea.' Seedlings are often inferior in color compared to cultivars.

Fall

Winter

Koelreuteria paniculata

kol-rih-TEE-ree-a pa-nik-u-LA-ta
Golden Raintree, Varnish Tree, Japanese Lantern Tree
Sapindaceae—Soapberry Family

❖

Deciduous Tree
HEIGHT: 20 to 30 feet
SPREAD: 25 to 35 feet

Illustration by
Sandie Howard

*Summer flowers are followed by unique
seedpods in fall.*

LANDSCAPE USE
Accent, specimen or focal interest for small landscapes. Good smaller tree for under power lines.

FORM
Spreading, ascending branches, with an open, rounded crown.

NATIVE RANGE
China, Korea, Japan. Introduced to the United States in 1763.

CHARACTERISTICS
FLOWER: 1/2-inch yellow flowers form on upright, pyramidal, loose airy clusters about 8 to 15 inches long in midsummer.

LEAVES: alternately spaced, pinnately compound about 14 inches long with 7 to 15 leaflets 1 to 3 inches long. The irregularly lobed, egg-shaped leaflets emerge as a purplish red, turning green as they mature and turning yellow in fall.

FRUIT: clusters of 3-parted, papery, lantern-shaped seedpods. Pods are 1 to 2 inches long; green, turning to tan; persisting through the winter. Seeds inside are pea-size, black.

BARK: light brown, furrowed on mature trees.

ROOT: deep.

CULTURE
SOIL: adaptable to a wide range. Tolerates alkalinity and low fertility levels.

EXPOSURE: full sun.

TOLERATES: air pollution; needs occasional pruning to remove dead or crossed branches, maintain shape and remove old flower panicles.

PROPAGATION: transplants best in the spring. Can be started from seed.

WATER: once established, will do well on low to moderate quantities. Watering into fall will keep plant from going dormant, thus reducing its winter hardiness and causing the roots to drown in heavy clay soils.

HARDINESS ZONES: 5 to 9.

LIFE SPAN: relatively short; 20 to 25 years.

BEST FEATURES
One of a few mid-summer flowering trees; paper lanterns in the fall extend its attractiveness.

COMPANION PLANTS
The purplish *Liatris punctata* (Dotted Gayfeather) and yellow or red of *Coreopsis tinctoria* (Coreopsis) will be flowering at about the same time.

DISADVANTAGES
Best growing success is attained at elevations below 6,000 feet in Colorado. In northern regions of the country, trees should be selected from stock originating from northern latitudes. Self-sows readily. (Many seedlings develop from dropped seedpods.) Subject to snow-load damage.

CULTIVARS
'Fastigiata'—narrow columnar habit. Fewer blooms and fruit than the common *K. paniculata* and much more prone to breakage.

Golden Raintree in late-summer garden.

Midsummer bloom.

◀ *Fall*

Winter

51

Speckled leaves and second-year hanging cone

Illustration by
Marie Orlin

Pinus aristata

PI-nus a-ris-TA-ta
Bristlecone Pine, Foxtail Pine
Pinaceae—Pine Family

❖

Alpine Conifer
HEIGHT: 20 to 30 feet
SPREAD: 10 to 15 feet

LANDSCAPE USE
Specimen, evergreen hedge,
parks, naturalization.

FORM
Trunk is short, stocky and
contorted; dense crown;
irregular spreading branches; shrubby
in appearance. More open as tree matures.

NATIVE RANGE
7,500- to 10,800-foot elevations in Colorado, Utah, Nevada and California. Can be established at lower elevations to 4,500 feet. Commonly seen at timberline, where it is shaped by the wind, contorted and is part of the "Krummholz."

CHARACTERISTICS
FLOWER: female is purple, male is dark orange-red; early spring, not particularly showy.
LEAVES: in clusters of 5; 1 to 1½ inches long, densely clustered along stems and branches; deep green; conspicuous, white resin flecks appear on needles; needles persist for 10 to 15 years.
FRUIT: shiny, dark brown, egg-shaped cones that have small prickles on the scales, giving this plant its name.

CULTURE
SOIL: rocky, poor soil, well drained. Tolerates alkalinity.
EXPOSURE: full sun.
TOLERATES: the wind.
PROPAGATION: sow seed in fall or early spring.
WATER: does well on little water, but does better with extra water during driest months of the summer. Can be induced to grow a little faster with supplemental water. Excessive water and poorly drained clay soils results in death or straggly growth.
HARDINESS ZONES: 2 to 6.
LIFE SPAN: very long.

New cones

Summer garden

BEST FEATURE
Beautiful 12 months of the year.

COMPANION PLANTS
Juniperus horizontalis 'Blue Chip' (Blue Chip Juniper), *Caryopteris* x *clandonensis* (Blue Mist Spirea) and ornamental grasses.

DISADVANTAGES
Does not withstand air pollution. Generally slow growing.

OTHER SPECIES
P. cembroides edulis (Piñon Pine)—20 to 30 feet tall, dense foliage, deep green, bushy to pyramid shaped. *P. flexilis* (Limber Pine)—30 to 50 feet tall, emerald green needles, open irregular or column-shaped crown, variable bark colors as it matures. *P. mugo* (Mugo Pine)—5 to 20 feet tall, dark green needles, dense broad, round or conical crown. *P. nigra* (Austrian Pine)—50 to 60 feet tall, open, broad, pyramidal crown, long, dark green needles; withstands city conditions.

Young Ponderosa in spring

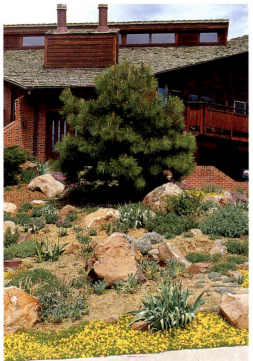

Pinus ponderosa

PI-nus pon-der-O-sa
Ponderosa Pine, Western Yellow Pine
Pinaceae—Pine Family

Conifer Tree
HEIGHT: 80 to 100 feet
SPREAD: 25 to 30 feet

LANDSCAPE USE
Native planting; mass or group plantings; windbreak or a focal point in the landscape.

FORM
Narrow, pyramidal, tightly packed with branches when young.
At maturity, it is massive, with irregular branching, forming an open crown and allowing light to filter through.

NATIVE RANGE
Found from Canada into Mexico and throughout the western United States and Texas. In Colorado, grows at 5,000- to 9,000-foot elevations.

CHARACTERISTICS
FLOWER: not significant except for pollen, which is yellow in color.
LEAVES: needles in clusters of 2 to 3 and 4 to 7 inches in length. Dark green to yellowish green. Three-year-old needles are shed annually.
FRUIT: cones, broad, egg-shaped, shiny, reddish brown and prickly to touch; 2 to 7 inches long.
BARK: brownish black on young trees; yellowish brown to cinnamon-red and broken into fissured plates on older trunks. On warm sunny days, mature trees' bark will emit a butterscotch odor.
ROOT: deep tap.

CULTURE
SOIL: prefers well drained, sandy or gravelly soil. Tolerates alkaline, clay soils where excellent drainage exists.
EXPOSURE: grows best in an open exposure with full sun but will tolerate some shade.
PROPAGATION: seed.
WATER: will do well with little water.
TOLERATES: drought, heat, prolonged wind and cold once established.
HARDINESS ZONES: 3 to 7.
LIFE SPAN: growth is slow the first decade but accelerates to about a foot a year thereafter. Maturity is about 350 to 500 years.

BEST FEATURES
Medium growth rate, good windbreak, attractive evergreen presence.

COMPANION PLANTS
Mahonia repens (Creeping Grape Holly), *Arctostaphylos uva-uvsi* (kinnikinnick) and *Symphoricarpus chenaultii* 'Hancock' (Hancock Coralberry).

DISADVANTAGES
Bark beetles, mistletoe and some fungi can cause problems but it is minimal in home landscapes. Pollen production can be heavy in some years.

Stems, leaves and mature cone.

Illustration by Marie Orlin

53

Potentilla fruticosa

po-ten-TIL-a froo-ti-KO-sa
Bush Cinquefoil, Potentilla; Shrubby Cinquefoil
Rosaceae—Rose Family

❖

Deciduous Shrub
HEIGHT: 1 to 4 feet
SPREAD: 2 to 4 feet

"Fruticosa" means shrubby or bushy.

Illustration by
Ann Lowdermilk

LANDSCAPE USE
Shrub border; mass planting; integrated into foundation plantings for long season of color; informal hedges; mixed perennial border.

FORM
Upright or arching stems densely covered with foliage, forming a low, rounded bush.

NATIVE RANGE
Widely distributed in the northern latitudes of the world on moist hillsides and meadows. At the lower latitudes in the United States, it is found in the mountainous regions around 6,000 to 10,000 feet.

CHARACTERISTICS
FLOWER: typically bright buttercup yellow and about 1 inch in size with 5 separate heart-shaped petals. New cultivars have variation of flower colors from white to orange. The bloom is the most showy at the first of the summer but will continue to have a reduced display until first frost. Flowers form only on new wood.
LEAVES: about 1-inch long, multi-lobed, slightly hairy, moderate to dark green.
FRUIT: rich brown seed heads are attractive in winter.
BARK: not significant.

CULTURE
SOIL: prefers fertile, well drained soils. However, it is adaptable to poor, alkaline, dry, clay soils.
EXPOSURE: full sun; extreme cold; partial shade okay, but flowering is reduced.
PROPAGATION: seed or softwood cuttings.
WATER: good drought tolerance; performs best when given additional moisture beyond natural precipitation.
TOLERATES: annual pruning to 6 or 8 inches.
HARDINESS ZONES: 2 to 7.

BEST FEATURE
Long blooming season and grows under a variety of conditions.

COMPANION PLANTS
Ephedra viridis (Green Mormon Tea) and *Sempervivum* spp. (Hens and Chicks).

DISADVANTAGES
Occasionally can get leaf spot or mildews. Spider mites can be a problem under hot, dry, dusty conditions, causing the leaves to become bronze in color. The plant becomes ragged with age unless pruned back periodically even to the ground.

CULTIVARS
Cultivars have a variety of bloom color and size, along with varying heights and widths. 'Coronation Triumph' (looks especially good under CSU trials); 'Abbotswood'; 'Buttercup'; 'Jackmanii' and others. The red cultivars such as 'Tangerine', 'Red Ace' and others tend to show faded flowers in Colorado's intense sunlight.

Long blooming border accent in summer garden.

Spring

◀ *Summer*

Fall

Winter

PRU-nus ar-MEN-e-ac-a
Apricot
Rosaceae—Rose Family

❖

Deciduous Tree
HEIGHT: 15 to 30 feet
SPREAD: 20 to 30 feet

Spring flowers

Illustrations by
Susan T. Fisher

Leaves and midsummer fruit

Apricot in spring garden.

LANDSCAPE USE
Small tree for small landscapes; excellent dappled shade source; outstanding early spring ornamental accent.

FORM
Handsome, wide spreading, rounded, open crown.

NATIVE RANGE
Western Asia. Good to 7,000 feet in Colorado.

◀ *Summer*

CHARACTERISTICS
FLOWER: single, white or pinkish, 1-inch diameter, covering the plant before the leaves emerge in early spring. Most are self-pollinating; some cultivars are not and need another cultivar nearby to fruit.
LEAVES: simple, alternate, fine-toothed, 3 to 4 inches long, almost as wide, bright green turning yellow in the fall.
FRUIT: edible, yellowish red, 1 to 2 inches in diameter.
BARK: attractive.

Fall

CULTURE
SOIL: prefers silty or clay loam, fertile and well drained. Tolerant of alkalinity.
EXPOSURE: full sun.
TOLERATES: dry heat, but not humid heat.
PROPAGATION: sow seed in the fall. Cuttings in late spring.
WATER: once established, does well on little supplemental water except in the driest months.
HARDINESS ZONES: 5 to 8.
LIFE SPAN: long.

Winter

BEST FEATURES
Spring flower, shade, fall color, winter branching structure.

COMPANION PLANTS
Amelanchier alnifolia (Saskatoon Serviceberry) and *Prunus besseyi* (Western Sand Cherry).

DISADVANTAGES
Susceptible to twig borer, thrips, peach crown borer and aphids. Early flower is susceptible to frost damage in colder climates, making fruit production unreliable.

OTHER CULTIVARS AND SPECIES
'Tilton', 'Sungold', 'Moongold', 'Moorpark' and many more. *P.a. mandschurica* (Manchurian Apricot)—performed well in Colorado State University studies; develops some red-orange-yellow fall leaf color. There are several dwarf varieties although they developed for fruit, not as ornamentals.

Prunus besseyi

PRU-nus BES-see-i
Western Sand Cherry, Hanson's Bush Cherry
Rosaceae—Rose Family

❖

Deciduous Shrub
HEIGHT: 4 to 6 feet
SPREAD: 4 to 6 feet

Early-spring flower

Midsummer stem, leaves and fruit

Illustration by
Ann Lowdermilk

Western Sand Cherry in fall landscape.

LANDSCAPE USE
Foundation plant, wildlife, massing, background border plant.

FORM
Spreading, open, airy, upright branches forming a rounded or vaselike shape.

NATIVE RANGE
Grasslands of eastern Colorado through western and central Kansas. Found among tall grasses, barren sandy areas or on rocky mesas. Will grow up to 8,000-foot elevations in Colorado.

CHARACTERISTICS
FLOWER: small clusters of white, fragrant flowers cover the plant in early spring.
LEAVES: narrow, oval, leathery, grayish green in summer, red in fall.
FRUIT: drupes are red when young, turning black and edible when ripe in midsummer.
BARK: reddish brown.
ROOT: *P. besseyi* has been used as "dwarfing rootstock" to create dwarf-size trees of peach, plum and apricot.

CULTURE
SOIL: sandy, clay, gravelly.
EXPOSURE: sun.
PROPAGATION: early summer cuttings; sow seed in the fall or stratify three months and plant seed in the spring.
WATER: dry to moist.
TOLERATES: pruning after flowering which is important to clean out weak or damaged stems.
HARDINESS ZONES: 4 to 7.
LIFE SPAN: short: 10 to 20 years.

BEST FEATURES
Spring flowers, clean foliage, red fall color, small size, roundish form.

COMPANION PLANTS
Ribes cereum (Wax Currant), *Artemisia frigida* (Fringed Sage) and *Antennaria* spp. (Pussytoes).

DISADVANTAGES
Some susceptibility to powdery mildew, borers crown and aphids. Tends to sucker if watered too much.

Spring

 Summer

Fall

Late winter

59

Prunus virginiana

PROO-nus ver-jin-e-A-na
Chokecherry
Rosaceae—Rose Family

Large Shrub or Small Tree
HEIGHT: 20 to 30 feet
SPREAD: 10 to 25 feet

*Two phases of
fruit color and the spring flower*

Illustration by
Angela Overy

LANDSCAPE USE
Useful as specimen when kept pruned or as a clump tree or large shrub. Also appropriate for hedging, screening, naturalizing and attracting wildlife.

FORM
Suckering tree or shrub with oval, rounded crown formed from erect branches and dense foliage.

NATIVE RANGE
Different variations of *P. virginiana* are widespread throughout the United States and generally located in the West in mountainous regions up to 10,000 feet.

CHARACTERISTICS
FLOWER: creamy white flowers hang in 5-inch-long racemes in mid-spring, covering the tree.
LEAVES: alternate, broad leaf, dark green above and grayish green below, 1 1/2 to 5 inches. Turning yellow or red in the fall depending upon variety.
FRUIT: red turning to purple in late summer; edible but sour, best used for jelly or syrup.
BARK: rough, speckled, red-brown to dark brown, many white lenticels.

CULTURE
SOIL: adaptable to low fertility and a wide range of textures.
EXPOSURE: sun.
PROPAGATION: sow seed in the fall, early summer cuttings.
WATER: dry to moderate.
HARDINESS ZONES: 2 to 6.
LIFE SPAN: short: 10 to 20 years.

BEST FEATURES
Drought tolerant and extremely hardy. Three seasons of interest considering flowers, fruit and leaf colors.

COMPANION PLANTS
Juniperus spp. (various Junipers) and *Potentilla fruticosa* (Shrubby Cinquefoil).

DISADVANTAGES
Suckering; browse for deer; subject to insects and disease.

CULTIVARS AND VARIETIES
'Shubert' (Shubert Chokecherry)—pyramid form with new green leaves turning to purple. 'Canada Red' is similar to 'Shubert'. *P. virginiana* var. *melanocarpa*—black fruit; native from the West Coast to the Rocky Mountains.

'Shubert' Chokecherry in summer landscape.

Spring flower and leaf color.

Summer

Fall

Winter

Quercus bicolor

KWER-kus BI-col-or
Swamp White Oak
Fagaceae—Beech Family

❖

Deciduous Tree
HEIGHT: 40 to 50 feet
SPREAD: 30 to 50 feet

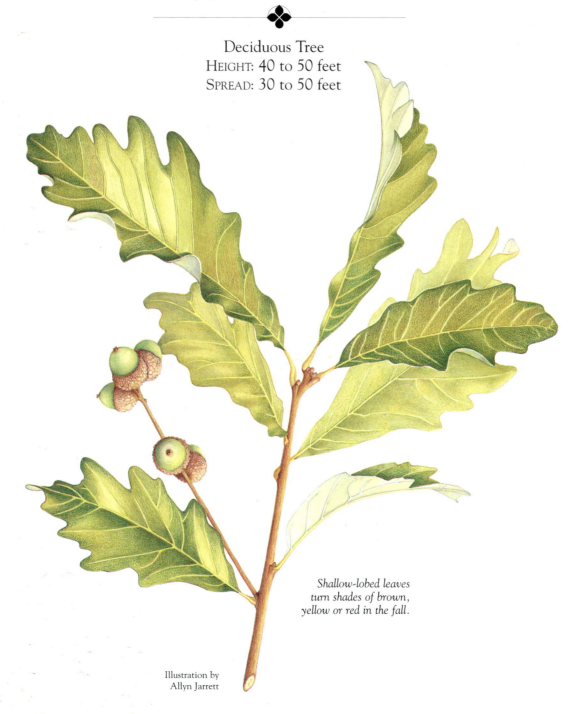

*Shallow-lobed leaves
turn shades of brown,
yellow or red in the fall.*

Illustration by
Allyn Jarrett

62

LANDSCAPE USE
Shade tree.

FORM
Lower branches on a short-trunked tree are descending while upper branches are more erect, creating a broad, somewhat open, conical to rounded crown. Medium texture in the landscape.

NATIVE RANGE
Quebec to Georgia and Arkansas; grows in moist bottomlands. In Colorado can be established up to 6,000-foot elevation.

CHARACTERISTICS
FLOWER: yellow-green and inconspicuous.
LEAVES: 4- to 8-inch rounded lobes, darker green top, lighter green to white and velvety underneath. Yellow to orange and red fall color.
FRUIT: acorns, 1-inch diameter, usually in pairs and abundant every 3 to 5 years.
BARK: pale, gray-brown, exfoliating when young and deeply furrowed at maturity.

CULTURE
SOIL: adaptable to most soil types, but like many oaks, prefers acidic soils. Once established, tolerates the low soil oxygen of heavy clay, compaction or poor drainage. Also tolerates saline soils.
EXPOSURE: sun to light shade.
PROPAGATION: seeds. Also can be transplanted more easily than other White Oaks.
WATER: wet to dry; drought tolerant.
HARDINESS ZONES: 4 to 7.
LIFE SPAN: very long.

BEST FEATURES
Handsome tree. Attractive fall color. Clay tolerant.

COMPANION PLANTS
Plants that enjoy heavy shade such as *Galium odoratum* (Sweet Woodruff) or *Lamium maculatum* (Spotted Dead Nettle).

DISADVANTAGES
Slow growing. Chlorosis occurs in alkaline soils. Probably best not to plant if pH is more than 7.5.

OTHER SPECIES
Quercus robur (English Oak)—similar in appearance and size but less tolerant of compacted soils; more tolerant of alkaline, soils. *Q. macrocarpa* (Burr Oak)—tolerant of alkaline clay soils.

Swamp White Oak in summer garden.

Spring

 Fall

Winter

Quercus macrocarpa

KWER-kus mak-ro-CAR-pa
Burr Oak
Fagaceae—Beech Family

Deciduous Tree
HEIGHT: 60 to 80 feet
SPREAD: 50 to 70 feet

Mossy cup acorns form in midsummer.

Illustration by
Allyn Jarrett

LANDSCAPE USE
Stately shade tree that is equally impressive for its beautiful foliage in summer and its structure in winter.

FORM
Young growth habit is variable; canopy becomes broad and spreading, creating a majestic tree with maturity.

NATIVE RANGE
From Nova Scotia to Texas and northwest to the Dakotas. Sites include moist rich bottomlands of the South and low dry hills of the Plains. Can be established up to 6,500 feet in Colorado.

CHARACTERISTICS
FLOWER: inconspicuous.
LEAVES: dark green and pale green underneath, bluntly lobed, about 4 to 10 inches in length, become yellow-brown in the fall.
FRUIT: acorn with the cup enclosing half of the nut with a fringelike border (also called Mossy Cup Oak).
BARK: dark gray corky bark develops deep ridges with age; especially beautiful in winter.

CULTURE
SOIL: adaptable to a wide range of soil types including alkaline.
EXPOSURE: full sun only.
PROPAGATION: seed.
WATER: adaptable to moist or dry conditions.
HARDINESS ZONES: 3 to 8.
LIFE SPAN: long.

BEST FEATURES
A tough tree that tolerates a wide range of conditions as well as urban pollution.

COMPANION PLANTS
An understory of *Mahonia repens* (Creeping Grape Holly) or *Rosa glauca* (Red Leaf Shrub Rose) would be appropriate since they are shade tolerant.

OTHER SPECIES
Quercus gambelii (Gambel Oak)— 15-30 ft., shrub or small tree, attractive deep green leaves. Good to 8,000 in Colorado.

DISADVANTAGES
May be difficult to transplant.

Forty-year-old Burr Oak in summer landscape.

 Summer

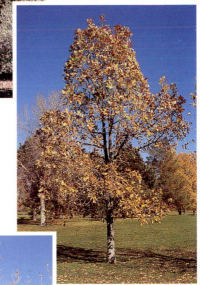

Fall

Winter

Rhus trilobata

rus tri-lo-BA-ta
Three Leaf Sumac, Skunkbush, Lemonade Sumac, Squawbush
Anacardiaceae— Cashew Family

Deciduous Shrub
HEIGHT: 3 to 6 feet
SPREAD: 3 to 6 feet

Ilustration by
Sandie Howard

*Male catkin (above) and fruit on
the same plant; fall and summer leaves*

LANDSCAPE USE

Dry shrub borders, barrier plantings or naturalistic settings. Appropriate for erosion control on difficult sites such as roadsides and steep banks. Plants sucker from the roots, forming a thick tangle of stems.

FORM

Rigid, arching branches form dense, round shrub.

NATIVE RANGE

West from Illinois to Washington and from California south to Texas; on dry, sunny foothills of the piñon-juniper zone. To 9,000 feet on steep mountain slopes.

CHARACTERISTICS

FLOWER: female flowers are not particularly showy, appear as yellowish green panicles at the end of the branches in spring before the leaves emerge. Preformed male catkins, attractive budlike structures, emerge by late summer, lasting through the winter, then elongate in April of the following year to release pollen.

LEAVES: glossy, dark green, divided into 3 egg-shaped lobes. Fall color is mottled with yellows, oranges and reds. Very mild skunklike odor when crushed.

FRUIT: small red or orange (berrylike) hairy drupe, develops in late summer, persisting into the winter, although its red color may fade. The edible fruit, with a slight lemon flavor, can be crushed and mixed with water and sugar to make a lemonadelike drink. Native Americans once dried the berries to be used in pemmican.

BARK: light brown. Native Americans used the young branches to weave baskets.

CULTURE

SOIL: adaptable to a wide range of soil types and conditions.

EXPOSURE: full sun to part shade.

PROPAGATION: sow seed in the fall or start from softwood cuttings in the spring or early summer.

WATER: one of the most drought tolerant sumacs, but will grow more vigorously with additional moisture.

HARDINESS ZONES: 4 to 7.

LIFE SPAN: long, moderate to rapid growth rate.

BEST FEATURES

It has an attractive fall color. It is very adaptable and is easily transplanted because of its fibrous root system. Attracts wildlife.

COMPANION PLANTS

Chrysothamnus nauseosus (Rabbitbrush) and *Chamaebatiaria millefolium* (Fernbush), grasses.

DISADVANTAGES

Leaves are considered malodorous by some people. Occasional problems with wilts, leaf spot, rusts, aphids, mites and scale but nothing serious. Attracts wildlife.

RELATED SPECIES OR CULTIVARS

R. aromatica (Fragrant Sumac)—its leaves tend to smell lemony when crushed. (Some botanists consider *R. trilobata* to be its western equivalent.) *R. aromatica* 'Autum Amber'—12-inch-tall groundcover form. *R. aromatica* 'Gro-low'—ground covering form to 18 inches tall. Nice yellow and reddish fall color.

Three Leaf Sumac in midsummer landscape.

Spring flower

◄ *Late summer*

Fall

Winter

67

Rhus typhina

roos ti-FE-na
Staghorn Sumac
Anacardiaceae—Cashew Family

❖

Deciduous Shrub
HEIGHT: 8 to 10 feet
SPREAD: 8 to 15 feet

*Leaves changing to fall
color with red panicle fruit.
Variety 'Laciniata'*

Illustration by
Sandie Howard

Staghorn Sumac in late summer garden

LANDSCAPE USE
Good for massing, banks, waste areas, naturalizing. Large planter boxes where it can sucker freely. Not recommended as a specimen or foundation plant.

FORM
Open, loose, spreading shrub with a flattish crown.

NATIVE RANGE
Quebec to Ontario, south to Georgia and Iowa. Can be established up to 7,500-foot elevations in Colorado.

CHARACTERISTICS
FLOWER: greenish yellow, hairy, dense, large terminal panicles from early to mid-summer.
LEAVES: 10 to 18 inches, bright green, finely dissected into oblong leaflets, each about 4 inches long. Fall color is rich in red, yellow and orange.
FRUIT: bright red late in summer to late fall. Dense hairy drupe.
STEMS: densely clustered, brown and hairy.

Mid-summer

CULTURE
SOIL: any well drained garden soil. Tolerates very dry, sterile soil.
EXPOSURE: rocky hillsides, sunny, and part shade.
PROPAGATION: seeds, root cuttings, transplanting and suckers.
WATER: drought tolerant.
HARDINESS ZONES: 4 to 8.
LIFE SPAN: long from rootstock.

◄ *Fall*

BEST FEATURES
Very showy fall foliage display. Dark red seed heads at ends of stems last many months and persist through winter. They also attract wildlife. Form beautiful large colonies.

COMPANION PLANTS
The dark green leaves can be contrasted with *Pennisetum setaceum* 'Rubrum' (Purple Fountain Grass) and with the low-growing *Mahonia repens* (Creeping Grape Holly).

DISADVANTAGES
When soil moisture is high, this plant is susceptible to chlorosis and will sucker more readily.

RELATED SPECIES OR CULTIVARS
'Laciniata'— with feathery, cut leaves. *R. glabra*— similar in growth habit, but with smooth stems, also tends to sucker more and shorter. *R. glabra* 'laciniata'— smooth stems and cut leaves. *R. glabra* var. *cismontana*— dwarfer form.

Winter

69

Robinia neomexicana

ro-BIN-e-a ne-o-mex-e-CAN-a
New Mexico Locust, Rose Locust
Fabaceae—Pea Family

Deciduous Shrub or Small Tree
HEIGHT: 6 to 20 feet
SPREAD: 10 to 20 feet

*New Mexico Locust is a showy ornamental
shrub with rose-pink flowers, coupled with
thorny stems.*

Illustration by
Marjorie C. Leggitt

LANDSCAPE USE

Beautiful flower; useful as windbreak or hedge. Favorable for stabilizing soil on hillsides.

FORM

Thicket-forming large shrub or small tree with irregular, rigid branches armed with paired thorns.

NATIVE RANGE

On foothill slopes and along roads from Texas to New Mexico and Arizona north to Colorado, Utah and Nevada up to 8,500 feet.

CHARACTERISTICS

FLOWER: pink or lavender drooping racemes emerge in early summer.
LEAVES: leaflets in 9 to 21 pairs, 1 inch long, elliptical, gray-green, rather colorless in the fall.
FRUIT: 4 inches, flat, hairy seedpods persist into winter.
BARK: black with spines.
ROOT: spreads by stolons, forming suckers.

CULTURE

SOIL: adaptable to any well drained soil types.
EXPOSURE: sun.
TOLERATES: pruning in early spring to shape and control size. Heat, drought and poor soil.
PROPAGATION: seed and cuttings.
WATER: dry to moderate.
HARDINESS ZONES: 4 to 8.
LIFE SPAN: moderate.

BEST FEATURES

Bloom is very showy; adapts well to adverse conditions. Doesn't need fertilization because it fixes nitrogen into the soil through its own root system.

COMPANION PLANTS

Pinus edulis (Piñon), *Juniperus scopulorum* (Rocky Mountain Juniper) and *Quercus gambelii* (Gambel Oak).

DISADVANTAGES

Suckers freely, especially when overwatered. Best to use in low-water, isolated areas. Overwatering will make it prone to borer damage.

RELATED SPECIES

R.pseudoacacia (Black Locust)—larger, eastern U.S. species that has naturalized in the Southwest. Black Locust is inferior as a landscape plant, however.

New Mexico Locust pruned to tree form in early summer landscape.

◄ *Early summer shrub form*

Fall

Winter

Sophora japonica

soh-FOR-ah ja-PON-i-ka
Japanese Pagoda Tree, Chinese or Japanese Scholar Tree
Fabaceae—Pea Family

❖

Deciduous Tree
HEIGHT: 40 to 60 feet
SPREAD: 40 to 60 feet

Illustration by
Karen Boggs

Late-summer flower

LANDSCAPE USE

Medium-sized tree, good for city conditions and poor soil. Useful in parks, lawns, golf courses. One of the few trees flowering in late summer.

FORM

Upward spreading branches that form an oval to rounded crown. Casts light shade.

NATIVE RANGE

China, Korea. Appropriate for elevations up to 6,000 feet in Colorado.

CHARACTERISTICS

FLOWER: 1/2 inch, yellow-white, pea-shaped in long clusters lasting several weeks during the end of summer. Flower clusters are as wide as they are long. Tree is very showy in flower and mildly fragrant. It is reported that flowering usually occurs after age 10, although it has been noted to bloom before that in Denver.

LEAVES: 7 to 9 inches long, compound, 1- to 2-inch leaflets, dark glossy green, oval or lance-shaped. Fall leaf is light yellow.

FRUIT: bright green pods changing to yellow and then yellow-brown, 2 to 8 inches long, persisting through winter.

BARK: trunk is grayish brown. Older trunks are deeply furrowed. New branches are green.

Spring

CULTURE

SOIL: does well in a variety of well drained soils.

EXPOSURE: sun. Will sunscald when young if not winter wrapped.

PROPAGATION: seeds; cultivars are budded.

WATER: once established can withstand drought.

HARDINESS ZONES: 5 to 8.

LIFE SPAN: long. (Some specimens in England are 200 years old.) Moderate growth rate at first, then slows.

BEST FEATURES

Beautiful tree in flower with wonderful foliage. Still a bit unknown, but becoming more available.

COMPANION PLANTS

Cerastium tomentosum (Snow in Summer) does well under light shade, and its gray leaves provide a nice contrast to the bright green of this tree.

Fall

DISADVANTAGES

Petal litter from the creamy white flowers may be objectionable to some. Possible diseases or insects include canker, twig blight, powdery mildew, scale and root rot, although they are usually not too serious. Winter dieback occurs, especially in exposed sites and on edges of suburbs. Cease water in later summer or early fall to improve winter survival. Subject to snow-load damage.

SUBSPECIES OR VARIETIES

S. japonica 'Pendula'—weeping form. *S. japonica* 'Regent'—supposedly less hardy, perhaps not usable at all in the Rocky Mountain region.

Winter

Spiraea x vanhouttei

spi-RE-a x van-HOOT-e-i
Vanhoutte Spirea
Rosaceae—Rose Family

Deciduous Shrub
HEIGHT: 6 to 8 feet
SPREAD: 5 to 10 feet

Illustration by
Linda Lorraine Wolfe

Spring flower, narrow, willowy stems with alternately placed leaves.

LANDSCAPE USE
Specimen plant, informal hedge or mass planting.

FORM
Fine-textured, medium-sized shrub with an elegant fountainlike shape.

NATIVE RANGE
The Vanhoutte Spirea is a cross between *S. trilobata* (native to central and eastern Asia) and *S. cantoniensis*, which is from China. Can be established up to 7,500 feet in elevation.

CHARACTERISTICS
FLOWER: numerous domed clusters of pure white blossoms grace the length of arching branches during late spring or early summer.
LEAVES: blue-green, egg-shaped, 1½ inches across. Fall color tends toward yellows and reds but isn't consistently showy.

CULTURE
SOIL: thrives in a variety of soils.
EXPOSURE: full sun to filtered shade; prefers open areas.
PROPAGATION: softwood cuttings.
WATER: adaptable to dry or moist conditions. Best flowering occurs with extra water and full sun.
HARDINESS ZONES: 4 to 7.
LIFE SPAN: long.

BEST FEATURES
One of the most popular spireas used in America due to its beautiful, spring flower displays and graceful fountainlike shape. Endures city conditions.

COMPANION PLANTS
Potentilla fruticosa (Potentilla) and *Buddleia alternifolia* (Fountain Butterfly Bush).

DISADVANTAGES
Susceptible to powdery mildew, aphids and scale. Requires some pruning to maintain attractive appearance and to keep in bounds. Prune (keeping the natural shape in mind) only in the spring after blooming to ensure a good display the following year.

CULTIVAR
S. x 'Renaissance' —touted as being more disease resistant. Several small species and hybrids, with a similar look, are available. These are excellent for smaller gardens. Example— 'Snowmound.'

Vanhoutte Spirea in spring garden

Spring

 Summer

Fall

Winter

75

Syringa vulgaris

si-RIN-gah vul-GA-ris
Common Lilac
Oleaceae—Olive Family

❖

Deciduous Shrub
HEIGHT: 8 to 20 feet at maturity
SPREAD: 6 to 15 feet at maturity

Spring flower on last year's growth.

Illustration by
Linda Evans

White and purple
Lilac in spring garden.

LANDSCAPE USE
Shrub borders, groupings, shelterbelts, specimens.

FORM
Strong multi-stemmed branches form an upright, vase-shaped or rounded shrub.

NATIVE RANGE
Europe to Asia; 4,000- to 11,000-foot elevations.

CHARACTERISTICS
FLOWER: pale purple; 6- to 10-inch, conical clusters form at the ends of the branches in late spring with an occasional bloom in the fall. Flowers form on new growth from the year before. Extremely fragrant.
LEAVES: 2 to 5 inches, bluish green, oval to heart-shaped, simple and opposite. Not noted for its fall color.
FRUIT: oval, 1/2- to 3/4-inch, brown capsule, which is not important ornamentally.

Spring

CULTURE
SOIL: basic, well drained. Amend with well rotted manure.
EXPOSURE: best in full sun and good air circulation to avoid or reduce powdery mildew. Avoid overcrowding.
PROPAGATION: softwood cuttings, grafts.
WATER: performs best with additional water but drought tolerant once established.
HARDINESS ZONES: 3 to 7.
LIFE SPAN: long.
PRUNING: prune immediately after blooming (sets buds on old wood). Prune out 1/4 to 1/3 of the oldest stems at base yearly for disease control and to improve sunlight entry into plant and to increase flowering.

 Late summer foliage

BEST FEATURES
Extremely fragrant; showy flowers in the spring; easily established.

COMPANION PLANTS
Tulips and Daffodils and other shrubs in a border.

DISADVANTAGES
Prone to some diseases and insects such as buck spot, brown spot, blight, gall, lilac-ash borer, oyster shell scale, leaf miner. Suckers, forming very overgrown clumps if not renewal pruned.

Fall

OTHER SPECIES AND CULTIVARS
More than 400 cultivars with flower colors ranging from white to pink to red to purple and blue.
S. *vulgaris* 'Alba'—white flowers. There are also many related species: S. *meyeri*, S. *patula*, S. *reticulata*, S. *villosa*, S. *pekinensis*, S. x *hyacinthiflora*, S. x *persica*, S. *oblata* v. *dilitata* ('Cheyenne') is resistant to deer browsing while S. *vulgaris* is browsed heavily where large deer populations exist.

Winter

Viburnum lantana

vy-BUR-num lan-TAN-a
Wayfaring Tree, Viburnum
Caprifoliaceae—Honeysuckle Family

❖

Deciduous Shrub
HEIGHT: 10 to 15 feet
SPREAD: 10 to 15 feet

*Spring flower and two phases
of late-summer fruit.*

Illustration by
Nancy Wilbur Nelson

Spring

Early summer

LANDSCAPE USE
Informal hedge, screen or in a mixed shrub or perennial border, specimen plant or shelterbelt.

FORM
Thick spreading branches forming a rounded profile, coarse winter appearance.

NATIVE RANGE
Europe and Western Asia; long history of cultivation. Will survive up to 8,000 feet in Colorado.

CHARACTERISTICS
FLOWER: 3- to 5-inch wide clusters of small, white belllike flowers; appear in spring for two weeks.
LEAVES: broadly oval, leathery, green leaves with gray undersides (2 to 5 inches long) with slight wrinkled appearance; maroon fall color persists into early winter.
FRUIT: berrylike fruit (drupe) is 1/3 inch, progressing from yellow to red and finally ripening in early fall to black; very attractive to birds. A second nearby plant will encourage more "berry" production.
BARK: light gray twigs and as branches mature, they become heavily lenticelled.

◄*Late summer*

CULTURE
SOIL: performs best in well drained, rich soils, but adaptable to calcareous, alkaline dry soils.
EXPOSURE: sun to part shade.
PROPAGATION: seeds, softwood cuttings.
WATER: low to moderate.
HARDINESS ZONES: 4 to 8.
LIFE SPAN: medium.

BEST FEATURES
Very easy to maintain and grow; fibrous root system makes it easy to transplant; fruit is attractive to wildlife; almost no susceptibility to diseases or pests.

Fall

COMPANION PLANTS
Kolkwitzia amabilis (Beauty Bush) and *Potentilla fruticosa* (Shrubby Cinquefoil).

DISADVANTAGES
Occasional chlorosis; "fishy" flower odor.

CULTIVARS
'Mohican' has a compact growth habit, 6 feet tall, with fruit ripening in midsummer to a red-orange, persisting for 4 weeks, which is longer by 1 to 2 weeks for the species; 'Rugosum' is distinguished by its handsome, dark leaves.

Wayfaring Tree in winter garden

Yucca species

YUCK-a
Agavaceae—Agave Family

Evergreen Shrub
HEIGHT: 1 to 7 feet
SPREAD: 1 to 4 feet

Illustration by
Susan Rubin

The showy flower belies the ominous leaves.

LANDSCAPE USE

An underused accent plant for a bold, dramatic touch in the dry landscape.

FORM

Large basal rosette with occasional flower spikes rising above the large pointed leaves.

NATIVE RANGE

Much of North America, most species inhabit arid locations like the desert Southwest. The ones listed below can be established up 8,500' in Colorado.

CHARACTERISTICS

FLOWER: depending upon the species, the flower spike may be very short and tucked in among the leaves or rise above several feet; bell shaped, usually white or cream-colored, often tinged with purple, more open at night than in the daylight, slight fragrance, will not bloom every year. Pollination depends on the yucca moth. Neither Yucca or the moth can complete its life cycle without the other.

LEAVES: tough, leathery, bluish green, sword-shaped. often with coarse fibers at leaf margins.

FRUIT: most commonly it is a dry capsule that is easily shaken by the wind.

CULTURE

SOIL: sandy, fast draining.

EXPOSURE: sun.

WATER: dry with occasional deep soaking.

PROPAGATION: sow seeds in the fall.

HARDINESS ZONES: variable depending on plants' origins.

LIFE SPAN: medium, although "pup" formation off the main rosette can make the clump long-lived.

BEST FEATURES

Characteristic plant of western-style landscape. Leaves were used by Indians and pioneers to make coarse rope and the roots to make soap. Good for hot, dry, sunny spots where it is difficult to establish vegetation.

COMPANION PLANTS

Artemisia tridentata (Big Sage),
Salvia sclarea (Clary Sage).

DISADVANTAGES

Leaves have sharp tips, use away from high traffic area such as sidewalks and driveways.

ILLUSTRATED SPECIES

Y. glauca (Soapweed)—early summer creamy flowers on 3 to 4 stalks, leaves are about 1–2' tall, narrow, sharp and gray-green, native to Colorado and the Rocky Mountain region. *Y. filamentosa* (Adam's Needle)—tolerates light shade, not as drought tolerant, southeast U.S. origin, white flowers in midsummer on stalks 4–7' tall above narrow, green leaves. *Y. Baccata* (Banana Yucca)—in early summer creamy white flowers emerge on 2' stalks among 2' leaves. Leaves are blue green, broad with fibrous margins. Fruit is more fleshy than other species and is edible although not particularly tasty. There are about 40 species but these three are the most commercially available yuccas for the high plains and foothill regions of the Rocky Mountains.

Banana Yucca in spring garden

Soapweed

Adam's Needle

Late-spring garden

Rosa x harisonii

ro-za HAR-i-son-e-i
Harison's Yellow Rose
Rosaceae—Rose Family

Deciduous Shrub
HEIGHT: 2 to 5 feet
SPREAD: 4 to 6 feet

LANDSCAPE USE
Areas of mass plantings, hedges, hillsides, specimen.

FORM
Upright arching branches, irregular shape. Medium texture.

NATIVE RANGE
Asia. Cross between *R. foetida* and *R. spinosissima*. Came to the West with the pioneers. Good up to the 9,000-foot elevations in Colorado.

CHARACTERISTICS
FLOWER: fragrant, 2 inches, bright yellow, semi-double blossoms cover the plant in late spring.
LEAVES: fine-textured, dark green, elliptical, double serrate.
FRUIT: showy black hips.
STEM: thorny.

CULTURE
SOIL: adaptable to fine soils and coarse soils; must be well drained.
EXPOSURE: sun.
PROPAGATION: division.
TOLERATES: cold.
WATER: low to moderate.
Quite drought resistant once established.
HARDINESS ZONES: 3 to 10.
LIFE SPAN: long.

BEST FEATURES
Low maintenance, easily adapted, hardy rose.

COMPANION PLANTS
Anchusa azurea (Italian Bugloss) and *Salvia officinalis* (Garden Sage).

DISADVANTAGES
Blooms only once per season in cold climates; blooms twice in warmer regions.

CULTIVAR
'Vorbergii'—many single, cream-colored flowers.
There are many other fine shrub and old garden roses available that are just as drought tolerant.

Referred to as the "Yellow Rose of Texas."

Illustration by
Marie Orlin

82

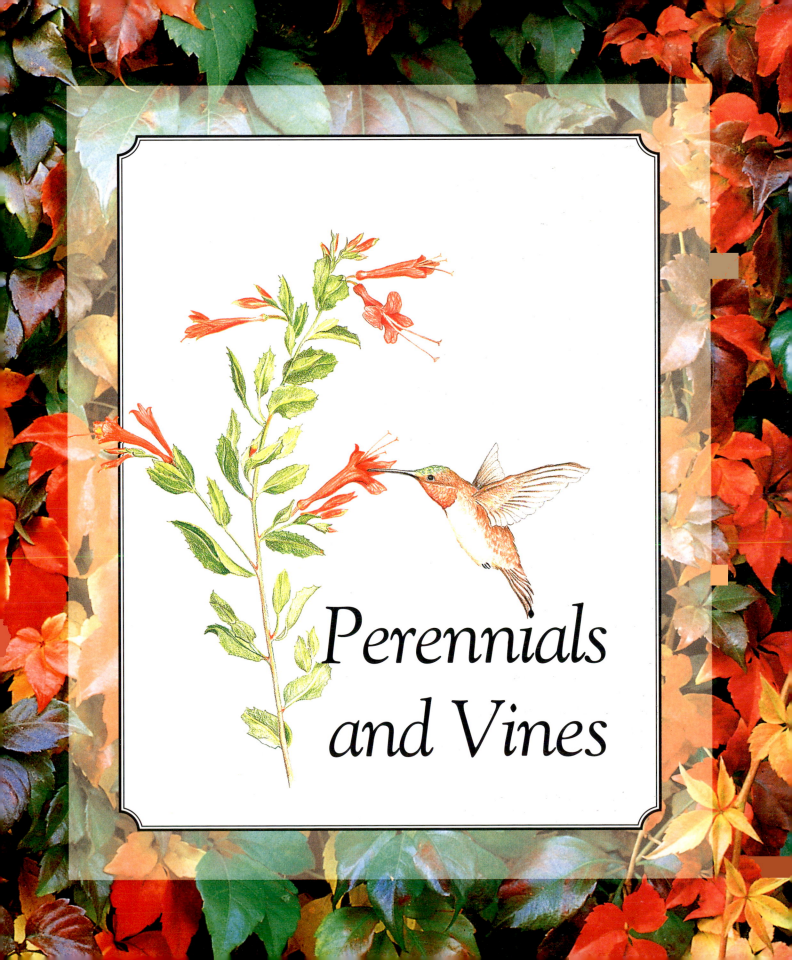

Perennials
and Vines

Achillea species

a-kil-LEE-a
Yarrow
Asteraceae—Sunflower Family

Herbaceous Perennial
HEIGHT: 2 inches to 4 feet
SPREAD: 6 inches to 3 feet

LANDSCAPE USE
Taller species are appropriate for massed plantings and mixed borders. The lower growing species look great in rock gardens or as a ground cover.

FORM
Stems are single or loosely clustered either as tall, stately plants or short and matlike.

NATIVE RANGE
Yarrows are found throughout the temperate Northern Hemisphere.
The 3 listed here can be established up to 9,000 feet in Colorado.

CHARACTERISTICS
FLOWER: yellow, gold, some white and diverse cultivars with colors of pink, red, lilac, cream, apricot and coral. Daisylike and closely packed into flattopped clusters at the ends of self-supporting stems. Long bloom period, which can be extended by deadheading.
LEAVES: alternate and growing all along the stem, finely dissected, woolly hairs, fernlike, gray or green, aromatic.
ROOT: weak rhizomes, some species forming clumps, others spreading to form large masses.

CULTURE
SOIL: adaptable to fertile as well as to poor, from sandy to clay, all well drained.
EXPOSURE: full sun.
PROPAGATION: divide clumps in spring or early fall; take cuttings in early summer; seeds may produce inferior plants.
WATER: moist to start and dry once established.
HARDINESS ZONES: 3 to 10.
LIFE SPAN: long because of their tendency to spread. Divide every 2 or 3 years to keep them within bounds.

Illustration by
Tana Pittman

A. tomentosa

A. millefolium

A. filipendula

Best Features

Long season of bloom; seed heads present nice winter appearance; some species can be mowed into a lawn; excellent cut or dried flowers; very drought hardy.

Companion Plants

Penstemons, Salvias, Daylilies. Bright flowers contrast well with deep green of *Miscanthus sinensis* (Miscanthus Grass) or *Cercocarpus ledifolius* (Curl-leaf Mountain Mahogany).

Disadvantages

Taller plants may need staking if excessively watered.

Highlighted Species

A. filipendula (Fernleaf or Tall Yellow Yarrow)—tallest of the yarrows, 2 to 4 feet, platelike yellow flower clusters 5 inches wide; early summer to early fall; 2 recommended cultivars are 'Coronation Gold' with bright yellow flowers and 'Moonshine' with pale lemon yellow flowers. *A. millefolium* (Common Yarrow)—1 to 3 feet tall, dark green leaves; the common white variety is considered weedy but there are recommended cultivars with a range of colors: 'Summer Pastels' with the full gamut of colors listed above and 'Rosea' with rose-pink flowers; midsummer to early fall. *A. tomentosa* (Woolly Yarrow)—forms fernlike mats 2 inches high with a spread of 2 feet, sporting bright yellow flowers in early and midsummer on 6-inch stems.

◀ *Common Yarrow maintained as a lawn.*

"Moonshine" Yarrow, *summer*

Tall Yellow Yarrow, *summer*

Late-summer garden

Agastache cana

ag-AH-sta-che CAN-a
Double Bubble Mint, Wild Hyssop,
Hummingbird's Mint, Mosquito Plant
Labiatae—Mint Family

❖

Herbaceous Perennial
HEIGHT: 2 to 3 feet
SPREAD: 1¹⁄₂ to 2 feet

Illustration by
Jill Sanders Buck

*Flowers provide a
pleasant fragrance.*

LANDSCAPE USE
Very showy perennial for sunny, dry, flower garden.

FORM
Bushy with branching stems from the ground, narrow leaves along the stems.

NATIVE RANGE
Western Texas and southern New Mexico, growing on dry slopes at high elevations in the mountains. 7,500 feet in Colorado.

CHARACTERISTICS
FLOWER: 1-inch, rose-purple, tubular flowers in late summer to early fall along top 12 inches of stem. Flowers have fragrance like Double Bubble Bubblegum.
LEAVES: very small, gray-green, aromatic, but with a different odor from the flowers.

CULTURE
SOIL: prefers well drained soil, overwatering is likely to be a problem if grown in clay.
EXPOSURE: warm, medium-dry position in full sun.
PROPAGATION: easily grown from seed.
WATER: low to medium.
HARDINESS ZONES: 3.
LIFE SPAN: long.

BEST FEATURES
Very showy, late-season color; flowers attract hawkmoths and hummingbirds over a long period of time; deer resistant.

COMPANION PLANTS
Hummingbird Flower, Ice Plants, Russian Sage.

DISADVANTAGES
Succumbs easily to root-rot if overwatered.

SUBSPECIES OR VARIETIES
A. *foeniculum* has blue flowers June through September; smells of aniseed and grows to 3 feet:
A. *barberi* grows to 4 feet or more, with larger, attractive blue-green felted leaves. It flowers earlier than A. *cana*, blooming mid- to late summer, and flowers are similar; leaves are rounded.

Spring garden

Alyssoides utriculata

al-ys-SOID-ees u-tric-u-LA-ta
Bladderpod
Brassicaceae—Mustard Family

Herbaceous Perennial
HEIGHT: 15 to 24 inches
SPREAD: 12 inches

LANDSCAPE USE
Dry banks, walls, rock gardens or dry borders. Easily grown for early spring color.

FORM
A basal rosette of leaves with flowers growing along the stem.

NATIVE RANGE
Inhabits rock and cliff crevices in the mountains of central Europe. Can be established up to 8,500 feet in Colorado.

CHARACTERISTICS
FLOWER: bright yellow flowers in early spring.
LEAVES: smooth to hairy evergreen rosettes.
FRUIT: inflated pod.

CULTURE
SOIL: well drained.
EXPOSURE: sun.
PROPAGATION: seed.
WATER: very low.
HARDINESS ZONES: 4 to 8.
LIFE SPAN: short, but reseeds.

BEST FEATURES
Similar to *Aurinia saxatile* (Basket of Gold), but larger flowered. The pods are long lasting and provide unusual summer texture.

COMPANION PLANTS
Iris spp. (Dwarf Bearded Iris) and *Lavendula* spp. (Lavender).

DISADVANTAGES
Reseeds vigorously, deadhead when pods are immature for use in dried arrangements and to prevent reseeding.

Summer seedpods

Illustrations by
Jill Sanders Buck

Spring flower with newly formed seedpods.

Spring flower

Spring garden

Anacyclus depressus

a-na-CY-clus dee-PRESS-us
Atlas Daisy
Asteraceae—Sunflower Family

Herbaceous Perennial
HEIGHT: 3 inches
SPREAD: 15 inches

*Closed flowers
with Snow-in-summer*

Illustration by
Shirley Nelson

LANDSCAPE USE
Good in dry rock gardens, front of dry borders, ground cover; especially attractive hanging over the edge of a wall.

FORM
Prostrate, dense.

NATIVE RANGE
Atlas Mountains, Morocco. Good to 10,000 feet in Colorado.

CHARACTERISTICS
FLOWER: stemless, white daisy in spring, closes when cloudy, revealing red undersides of petals.
LEAVES: grayish, finely cut.

CULTURE
SOIL: stony, well drained.
EXPOSURE: sun.
PROPAGATION: seed.
WATER: drought tolerant; needs occasional deep soaking.
HARDINESS ZONES: 3 to 10.
LIFE SPAN: individual plants may not be long-lived, but new seedling plants will keep the patch going.

BEST FEATURES
Soft, silvery green foliage is attractive even when this plant is not in bloom.

COMPANION PLANTS
Iris spp. (Bearded Iris), *Linum perenne* (Blue Flax) and *Veronica* sp.

DISADVANTAGES
Can reseed invasively in rich or well watered soils; deadhead to control spread.

Provides a soft, feathery appearance in the landscape

Midsummer flower

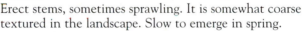
Silky seeds in early fall

Seedpods in late summer

Asclepias tuberosa

as-KLEP-e-us tube-a-RO-sa
Butterfly Weed, Gay Butterfly
Pleurisy Root, Orange Milkweed
Asclepiadaceae—Milkweed Family

Herbaceous Perennial
HEIGHT: 1 to 1 ½ feet
SPREAD: 1 to 2 feet

LANDSCAPE USE
Appropriate for very dry, sunny landscapes. Establishment on south-facing slopes or in remote traffic islands where watering is impractical will not deter this plant from producing a show. Placed in mixed borders, it is especially attractive with blue flowers.

FORM
Erect stems, sometimes sprawling. It is somewhat coarse textured in the landscape. Slow to emerge in spring.

NATIVE RANGE
5,000- to 7,000-foot elevations in Colorado. Found in meadows and canyons of Utah, Colorado, New Mexico and Arizona in the West and ranges as far northeast as Ohio down to Mississippi in the South.

CHARACTERISTICS
FLOWER: midsummer bloom lasts 2 to 4 weeks. Color is generally bright orange but varies between yellow and red, forming terminal clusters or cymes at the tips of the stems. Flower spikes are more numerous each year.
LEAVES: dark green sheen. Narrow and pointed to about 4 ½ inches. Thickly clustered along stems.
FRUIT: long, pointed; beige seedpods filled with silky hairs are used in fresh or dried arrangements.
STEMS: not milky.
ROOT: long and tuberous, making it difficult to transplant.

CULTURE
SOIL: well drained, sandy.
EXPOSURE: sunny.
TOLERATES: wind, heat, drought and poor soil.
PROPAGATION: sow in spring; need long days (13 or more hours) of light to germinate and grow. Use root division in the spring.
HARDINESS ZONES: 3 to 8.
LIFE SPAN: long; flowers the first season.

BEST FEATURES
Considered the most showy of all the native milkweeds. As the name indicates, it attracts butterflies, particularly some species of swallowtails and monarchs.

COMPANION PLANTS
Calamintha grandiflora (Calamint) and *Catananche caerulea* (Cupid's Dart).

DISADVANTAGES
Sometimes defoliated by butterfly larvae, but does not hurt plant. It is susceptible to aphid attack and powdery mildew.

Summer flower, fall pods.

Illustration by
Lori Rhea Swingle

89

Spring garden

Spring flower

Aurinia saxatile

(Formerly *Alyssum saxatile*)
aw-RI-nee-a sax-A-till-e
Basket-of-gold
Brassicaceae—Mustard Family

❖

Perennial
HEIGHT: 6 to 18 inches
SPREAD: 6 to 12 inches

Summer

LANDSCAPE USE
Effective around rocks as in a rock garden, along walls or bordering a rock pathway. Hard-to-water locations such as steep hillsides. Very showy planted in mass as a ground cover.

FORM
Loose clumps or hummocks of grayish green leaves. Framework of plant does not dieback like a normal perennial.

NATIVE RANGE
The Mediterranean region. Viable to 9,000 feet in Colorado.

CHARACTERISTICS
FLOWER: tiny, cross-shaped, bright yellow flowers are arranged in dense clusters, which cover the plant in early spring. Fragrant.
LEAVES: 2 to 5 inches long, slightly fuzzy with wavy edges; basal leaves longer than stem leaves. To keep plant from becoming too rangy and to reduce self-seeding, cut back and shape immediately after flowering.
ROOT: deep, woody taproot.

CULTURE
SOIL: prefers sandy and infertile, but will do fine in other soils as long as they are well drained. The clump tends to open up and sprawl if the soil is too rich.
EXPOSURE: full sun.
PROPAGATION: easy to start from seed.
WATER: low to moderate.
HARDINESS ZONES: 4 to 10.
LIFE SPAN: long.

BEST FEATURES
Low maintenance. One of the earliest and exceptionally showy flower displays in the spring.

COMPANION PLANTS
Spring bulbs, *Phlox subulata* (Creeping Phlox), *Iberis* and Lavender.

DISADVANTAGES
Attracts a few cabbage butterflies as do many related plants of the mustard family (a minor problem). Becomes rangy if not pruned regularly.

OTHER CULTIVARS
'Compactum'—tight, compact form, 10 to 12 inches high; 'Citrina'—pale yellow flowers. 'Gold Dust'—covered with bright yellow flowers. 'Dudley Neville'—pale yellow flowers.

Illustration by
Allyn Jarrett

Airy flowers above gray foliage.

Spring

Summer garden

Callirhoe involucrata

cal-li-RO-ee in-vol-u-CRAA-ta
Wine cup, Poppy Mallow,
Purple Poppy Mallow, Low Poppy Mallow
Malvaceae—Mallow Family

❖

Herbaceous Perennial Ground Cover
HEIGHT: 6 to 12 inches
SPREAD: 1 to 3 feet

LANDSCAPE USE
Lovely perennial for sunny
dry flower beds (covers nicely
around larger plants) and for
rock gardens; hangs over
walls or along the edge
of raised beds.

FORM
Low mat of 1- to 3-foot-long trailing stems.

NATIVE RANGE
Dry areas from Canada to Mexico and from Minnesota to Utah up to 6,000 feet.

CHARACTERISTICS
FLOWER: reddish purple, cup-shaped blooms with creamy white centers appear from early summer to early fall.
LEAVES: rich green, circular in shape and deeply cut, growing along the length of the trailing stems.
The leaves have a pleasant taste.
ROOT: deep tap. Reportedly has a sweet potato taste.

CULTURE
SOIL: dry, well drained.
EXPOSURE: full sun.
PROPAGATION: transplant seedlings in the spring
or purchase from nursery.
WATER: low water requirements but moderate
levels are tolerable if soil is well drained;
too much moisture causes a bare center
and a huge plant.
HARDINESS ZONES: 4 to 8.
LIFE SPAN: long.

BEST FEATURE
Long season of flower.

COMPANION PLANTS
Poppy Mallow is striking when planted with
the blue of *Perovskia atriplicifolia* (Russian Sage)
or interwoven with other ground covers
or other perennials such as Lamb's Ear.

DISADVANTAGES
None.

Illustration by
Tanya McMurtry

Trailing stems form a
ground cover, supporting flowers all summer.

Late summer

Garden in late summer

Campanula rotundifolia

kam-PAN-you-lah ro-tun-di-FOH-le-a
Bluebell, Harebell, Bluebells-of-Scotland
Campanulaceae—Bellflower Family

Herbaceous Perennial
HEIGHT: 6 to 12 inches first year; older plants up to 24 inches, but lax and sprawling
SPREAD: 8 inches first year, sprawls

Illustration by
Nancy Wilbur Nelson

LANDSCAPE USE
Naturalized areas, perennial borders, rock gardens.

FORM
Delicate clumps.

NATIVE RANGE
Foothills to tundra throughout the northern hemisphere.

CHARACTERISTICS
FLOWER: nodding 1-inch, lavender-blue, bell-shaped flowers early summer to early fall.
LEAVES: basal leaves are roundish; leaves on wiry stems are narrow, grasslike.

CULTURE
SOIL: tolerant of most soil conditions.
EXPOSURE: full sun, part shade, shade.
PROPAGATION: divisions, seeds (sow anytime, don't cover seed, germinates at 70°F).
WATER: low to medium.
HARDINESS ZONE: 1 to 10.
LIFE SPAN: best to remove older (2- to 3-year-old) plants and enjoy the younger volunteer seedlings.

BEST FEATURES
Self-seeds with abandon, resulting in dainty little bluebells springing up throughout plantings. Very long bloom season.

COMPANION PLANTS
In shady naturalized areas, use *C. rotundifolia* to punctuate low ground covers like *Veronica liwanensis* or *Penstemon* 'Claude Barr'. In perennial beds, let it self-seed around plants such as Dianthus, Coreopsis, white or blue Carpathian Harebell and Daisies.

DISADVANTAGES
Spent flowers turn brown, giving older plants a brown appearance if not regularly deadheaded; older plants get very leggy, sprawling over their neighbors and need to be cut to the ground or removed.

SUBSPECIES OR VARIETIES
Cultivar 'Olympica' has bright blue flowers and grows 12 to 18 inches.

Bluebells of Scotland

Early-summer garden

Centranthus ruber

sen-TRAN-thus RU-ber
Red Valerian, Jupiter's Beard, Fox Brush
Valerianaceae—Valerian Family

❖

Herbaceous Perennial
HEIGHT: 2 to 3 feet
SPREAD: 18 to 24 inches

Illustration by
Allyn Jarrett

LANDSCAPE USE
Showy plant for low and moderate water zones. Long blooming, attractive perennial for a flower bed.

FORM
Bushy clump.

NATIVE RANGE
Mediterranean region. Can be established up to 9,000 feet in Colorado.

CHARACTERISTICS
FLOWER: $^1/_2$ inch in size, forming terminal clusters of small trumpets. The flower varies in color from reddish pink or crimson to pale red. The flower is fragrant, and the blooming season is late spring and again in mid to late summer. *C.r.* 'Alba' is white.
LEAVES: 4 inches in length and have a bluish green color. The leaf is oval-shaped and has a smooth, waxy surface.
FRUIT: one seeded nut with a "tail."

CULTURE
SOIL: adaptable to dry soil; does well in any well drained soil.
EXPOSURE: full sun to part shade.
PROPAGATION: seed and division.
WATER: low to moderate water required.
HARDINESS ZONES: 3 to 9.
LIFE SPAN: short if overwatered.

BEST FEATURES
Showy plant; attracts butterflies; good source for cut flowers.

COMPANION PLANTS
Gaillardia x *grandiflora* 'Burgundy' (Blanket Flower), *Penstemon* spp.

DISADVANTAGES
Numerous seeds are produced and requires deadheading to impede spread.

Frequent removal of spent flowers can provide continuous summer bloom.

Campsis radicans

KAMP-sis RAD-i-kanz
Trumpet Vine, Common Trumpet Creeper
Bignoniaceae—Trumpet-creeper Family

❖

Deciduous Vine
HEIGHT: 30 feet
SPREAD: 30 feet, depends on support and structure

Late-summer flower, leaves and stem

Illustration by
Susan Rubin

Trumpet Vine in summer garden

LANDSCAPE USE
Covers stone walls, tree trunks and stumps, fences, pergolas and lath structures. Attracts butterflies.

FORM
Vine climbs via aerial roots which cling to most materials.

NATIVE RANGE
Pennsylvania to Missouri; Florida to Texas. Will survive to 5,500 feet in Colorado.

CHARACTERISTICS
FLOWER: funnels of orange and scarlet, $2\frac{1}{2}$ to 3 inches long, in clusters of 4 to 12 flowers; blooms in mid-summer; because flowers appear on current season's shoots, prune in early spring.
LEAVES: compound leaf composed of 9 to 11 leaflets, each 6 to 15 inches long; coarsely toothed. Yellowish green in fall.
FRUIT: 3-to 5-inch beanlike capsules.
STEMS: woody with light brown coloring.
ROOT: will start new plant where aerial roots contact soil.

CULTURE
SOIL: well drained; aggressive in rich soils.
EXPOSURE: best in full sun.
PROPAGATION: cuttings, division suckers and seed.
WATER: water to get established and then very drought tolerant.
HARDINESS ZONES: 5 to 9.
LIFE SPAN: long; slow to establish, vigorous thereafter.

BEST FEATURES
Attractive flower that is long lasting. Grows quickly to cover wall or fence.

COMPANION PLANTS
Zinnia grandiflora (Golden Paperflower)—a ground cover with yellow flowers and *Zauschneria arizonica* (Hummingbird Flower)—a red flowering perennial; both flower during the same time as the Trumpet Vine.

DISADVANTAGES
Suckering is a problem, but can be controlled by cutting roots with a spade. Due to the weight of mature vine, needs solid support structure. Aerial roots (holdfasts) on stems will damage wooden walls; makes painting difficult. Occasional problems with powdery mildew, plant hoppers and scale though usually not serious.

CULTIVARS
'Flava' has soft, butter-yellow flowers; 'Praecox' blooms red in spring; 'Atropurpurea' sports deep scarlet trumpets; 'Minor' is less vigorous with smaller flowers. All are hard to find and not as hardy as the species.

◀ *Summer*

Fall

Winter

Summary garden

Eriogonum umbellatum

e-ri-OG-o-num um-bel-LAT-um
Sulphur Flower
Polygonaceae—Buckwheat Family

Perennial Subshrub
HEIGHT: 6 to 12 inches
SPREAD: 1 to 2 feet

LANDSCAPE USE
Ground cover for a dry, sunny flower garden. Well suited for rock gardens and dry banks.

FORM
Broad loose mats.

NATIVE RANGE
Along the eastern Rocky Mountains and northwestern and southwestern mountains of the United States to timberline.

CHARACTERISTICS
FLOWER: flowers grow in ball-like umbels (clusters) on leafless stalks 4 to 12 inches tall. The pale to vibrant yellow flowers bloom from early to midsummer. Flowers age to a rust color and are useful in dried arrangements.
LEAVES: spatula-shaped leaves, dark green above and woolly below, create a rosette at base of plant. Forms evergreen or purplish mats in the winter.

CULTURE
SOIL: loose, gravelly well drained.
EXPOSURE: full sun.
PROPAGATION: seeds (self-sowing); division best when plants are small.
WATER: once established, very little water is needed.
HARDINESS ZONES: 3 to 8.

BEST FEATURES
Very drought tolerant, withstanding wind, spreads slowly by self-sowing. The vibrant yellow flowers can bring life and brightness to a garden.

COMPANION PLANTS
Asclepias tuberosa (Butterfly Weed) and *Centaurea cyanus* (Bachelor's Button).

DISADVANTAGES
May require some pruning to keep it compact; availability somewhat limited.

VARIETIES OR RELATED SPECIES
E. umbellatum var. *majus* (Subalpine Buckwheat)—flowers white to pale yellow, turning rose in late season.
E. ovalifolium (Cushion Eriogonum)— mat-forming; fuzzy leaves; yellow, cream or pink flowers.
E. niveum—white to light pink.
E. jamesii—white with silver leaves.

Leaves close to the ground minimize exposure to the drying wind.

Illustration by
D. Brown Tejada

96

Gaillardia aristata

gay-LARD-e-a a-ris-TA-ta
Blanketflower
Asteraceae—Sunflower Family

❖

Herbaceous Perennial
HEIGHT: 2 to 3 feet
SPREAD: 2 to 3 feet

Late summer garden

Fall

Winter

Illustration by
Marie Orlin

LANDSCAPE USE
Dry meadows, beds and
borders. Plant in groups
of 3 or more for impact.

FORM
Clump, with erect to spreading stems.

NATIVE RANGE
Hills and plains, in the western United States
at 5,000- to 9,000-foot elevations in open meadows.

CHARACTERISTICS
FLOWER: yellow with red centers, blooms all summer, good cut flower.
LEAVES: hairy, lance-shaped, green and primarily at the base of the plant with flower stems
extending above.

CULTURE
SOIL: light, open soil of poor to average fertility, won't tolerate heavy, wet soil in winter.
EXPOSURE: full sun.
PROPAGATION: division recommended every 3 years. Seed in spring or fall. Self-sows readily.
TOLERATES: heat and neglect.
WATER: dry, too much water will cause plant to flop.
HARDINESS ZONES: 3 to 8.
LIFE SPAN: short.

BEST FEATURES
Vigorous; easy perennial; flowers first year from seed. Showy all summer.

COMPANION PLANTS
Chrysothamnus nauseosus (Rabbitbrush), *Achillea* spp. and *Artemisia* spp.

DISADVANTAGES
Reseeds, but seedlings won't usually be true to type. Most of the seed or plants sold under this
name are actually hybrids, not the native species. Requires deadheading regularly to maintain a
tidy appearance and more flowers.

SPECIES OR VARIETIES
G. x *grandiflora* 'Burgundy'—solid wine red flower. G. x *grandiflora* 'Goblin'—red petals
with yellow tips and a red center; dwarf version. G. x 'Dazzler'—tall; red petals with yellow tips
and red center.

*Spent flower,
flower and
bud*

97

Late summer

Gutierrezia sarothrae

Late-summer garden

gut-er-REE-zia sa-ROTH-ree
Snakeweed, Broom Snakeroot, Matchweed,
Matchbush, Broomweed, Turpentine Weed
Asteraceae—Sunflower Family

❖

Perennial Subshrub
HEIGHT: 12 to 18 inches
SPREAD: 12 to 18 inches

Illustration by
Susan Rubin

LANDSCAPE USE
Attractive in shortgrass meadows, borders.

FORM
Low and bushy, somewhat woody at the base.

NATIVE RANGE
Open, dry plains and hills of Saskatchewan, south to Kansas, Mexico and
California. Found at 4,000- to 10,000-foot elevations in Colorado.

CHARACTERISTICS
FLOWER: small yellow, totally covering the plant from late summer to early fall.
LEAVES: bright green, alternate, narrow with smooth margins and
growing along full length of stem. Considered evergreen in
New Mexico and Arizona and deciduous in northern states.
FRUIT: oval and covered with chaffy scale.
STEMS: grow from crown each year, not from old growth.
They are stiff and somewhat resinous.

CULTURE
SOIL: poor, dry.
EXPOSURE: sun.
WATER: very drought tolerant.
PROPAGATION: seed.
HARDINESS ZONES: 4 to 6.
LIFE SPAN: long.

BEST FEATURES
Matchlike heads have been used as a treatment for snake bites;
dried stems have been bundled to make primitive brooms.

COMPANION PLANTS
Clumps of *Bouteloua gracilis* (Blue Gramma Grass), *Eriogonum umbellatum* (Sulfur Flower),
Ratibida columnifera (Prairie Coneflower) and *Penstemon spp.*

DISADVANTAGES
Extremely aggressive; can be invasive on rangelands; occasionally poisonous to grazing livestock,
but more commonly causes spontaneous abortions of livestock fetuses. Weedy in gardens, if not deadheaded.

SUBSPECIES OR VARIETIES
None.

*Narrow leaves of this plant are
an adaptation to dry conditions.*

Summer garden

Hemerocallis species

hem-er-o-KAL-is
Daylily
Liliaceae—Lily Family

❖

Herbaceous Perennial
HEIGHT: 1 to 6 feet, (usually about 3½ feet)
SPREAD: 1 to 3 feet

LANDSCAPE USE
Versatile. Plant in mass, in mixed borders, on slopes as a tall ground cover, as an informal hedge or in a cluster as specimen plants.

FORM
Large clumps of arching bladelike leaves with flower stems rising above the clump.

NATIVE RANGE
Japan and China. All will do well up to 8,000 feet in Colorado. Some will go up to 10,000 feet.

CHARACTERISTICS
FLOWER: variable sizes, ranging from 2 to 6 inches. Bell- or funnel-shaped. There is a range of solid colors from white, yellow, gold, pink to red and others that are multicolored. Varieties have either single or double blossoms, some with ruffled edges. The bloom season extends from spring to fall, depending on the variety. Bloom period varies among varieties from a couple of weeks to a couple of months. Each blossom dies at the end of the day but is replaced by another the next day.
LEAVES: green, narrow, sword-shaped and arching from the base of the plant, 1 to 2 feet long and 1/2 to 1 inch wide.

CULTURE
SOIL: well drained, with high organic matter.
Overfertilizing results in poor blooms and excess foliage.
EXPOSURE: full sun. In hot climates prefers partial shade.
PROPAGATION: divide root clumps every 2 to 6 years in late summer or fall. Stratify seeds for 6 weeks then germinate at 60° to 70° F.
WATER: moderately drought tolerant. Extra water prevents leaf scorch.
HARDINESS ZONES: 4 to 10.
LIFE SPAN: Cut leaves and stems to ground level each year in late summer or fall to clean up the garden.

BEST FEATURES
Daylilies have edible blossoms and are attractive to butterflies.
Continuous bloom throughout the summer can be achieved by selecting various cultivars.

COMPANION PLANTS
Linum perenne (Blue Flax) and *Achillea millefolium* (Yarrow, 'Summer Pastels').
Gaillardia spp and *Agstache* spp.

SUBSPECIES OR VARIETIES
There are thousands of cultivars and hybridized forms from the original 7 or so species. 'Stella de Oro' has gold flowers, is 12 inches tall and has the longest bloom period.

Today's flower was yesterday's bud.

Illustration by
Linda Lorraine Wolfe

Iris hybrids

I-ris
Bearded Iris, German Iris, Flag, The Rainbow Flower, Poor Man's Orchid
Iridaceae—Iris Family

◆

Perennial
HEIGHT: leaves are 1¹/₂ feet tall, while flower
stems can reach from 2 to 3 feet
SPREAD: 1¹/₂ to 2 feet or more

Illustrations by
Ann Lowdermilk

Blue and yellow are only a sample of the many colors available.

LANDSCAPE USE

As an accent plant along the border or fences and walls, in rock gardens and for early color after spring flowering bulbs have finished.

FORM

Clumps of erect swordlike leaves arranged in a fanlike pattern with stems and flowers rising above.

NATIVE RANGE

Probably originated from the Mediterranean region. Will grow up to the 8,500 foot elevations in Colorado.

CHARACTERISTICS

FLOWER: the flower consists of 6 petals: 3 inner "standards" that are erect and arching and 3 outer "falls" that droop. Each fall has a distinct beard resembling a hairy caterpillar. The standards and falls can reach 3 inches or more in length.

Iris in a perennial border

The Bearded Iris has a wide range of flower colors: black, violet, purple, blue, brown, orange, yellow, white and cream. They are often bicolored. Some varieties are fragrant. Their bloom cycle is late spring and early summer.

LEAVES: swordlike, bluish green, about 2 inches wide.

CULTURE

SOIL: well drained soils; plant rhizomes shallow as they prefer growing near the surface and will withstand considerable drying and exposure.

EXPOSURE: full sun.

PROPAGATION: rhizome division; choose rhizomes with a strong fan; plant after flowering and before August.

WATER: will endure drought conditions.

HARDINESS ZONES: 4 to 9.

LIFE SPAN: long.

BEST FEATURES

This easy-to-grow perennial is attractive in leaf. Flowers come in a rainbow of colors ("iris" is Greek for "rainbow"). Can tolerate drought.

◄ *Spring*

COMPANION PLANTS

Phlox subulata (Creeping Phlox) and *Aurinia saxtile* (Basket of Gold).

DISADVANTAGES

Occasionally attacked by iris borer. The foliage will dominate a bed after flowering, so use cautiously as an accent.

SUBSPECIES OR VARIETIES

At one time, Bearded Iris was named *Iris germanica* (German Iris). However, Iris are of complicated and sometimes obscure parentage.

Summer and fall appearance

Fall seed heads▼

Late-summer bloom ▲

Liatris punctata

li-a-tris punk-TA-ta
Gayfeather, Dotted Gayfeather, Cachana, Blazing Star
Asteraceae—Sunflower Family

Herbaceous Perennial
HEIGHT: 6 to 24 inches
SPREAD: 12 to 18 inches

LANDSCAPE USE
Bank cover among warm season grasses; accent in beds and borders; foundation plantings where water is to be held to a minimum.

FORM
Erect, airy, narrow stems arise from a basal tuft of narrow grasslike leaves.

NATIVE RANGE
Western native in the mid-grass prairie as far north as Manitoba, Canada, south to Texas, west to northeastern New Mexico, between 5,000- to 8,000-foot elevations.

CHARACTERISTICS
FLOWER: bright pink-lavender. 6-inch spike at top of stem, blooms from the top down. Blooms are in their prime from 2 to 4 weeks in mid to late summer. To extend blossom time, remove center flower spikes as flowers fade, and lateral spikes will flower.
LEAVES: narrow, grasslike, smooth, gray-green and dotted. Basal leaves are about 4 inches long, becoming shorter the higher they are situated on the flower stalk.
FRUIT: decorative in winter; self-sows.
ROOT: deep, tuberous taproot.

CULTURE
SOIL: prefers infertile, dry, gravelly, shallow soil; grows compactly under these conditions. In richer, moist soil, may become more rangy.
EXPOSURE: full sun.
PROPAGATION: sow seed anytime. Easy to transplant.
TOLERATES: winter conditions, dry soil, cold, low humidity, heat and mowing after seed heads brown.
WATER: low, 14 to 16 inches per year.
HARDINESS ZONES: 3 to 5.
LIFE SPAN: long; persistent; moderate growth rate.

BEST FEATURES
Bright, intense pink-lavender spike attracts butterflies and bees. Long lasting cut or dried flowers. Not usually browsed by deer.

COMPANION PLANTS
Foliage blends with other blue-toned foliage such as *Bouteloua gracilis* (Blue Grama Grass) and tawny golden grass foliage such as *Sorghastrum nutans* (Yellow Indian Grass) in meadows. Contrasts with silver foliage of *Artemisia frigida* (Silver Fringed Sage) and the light, airy seed heads of *Oryzopsis hymenoides* (Indian Rice Grass).

DISADVANTAGES
Slow to establish.

SPECIES OR VARIETY
Liatris spicata—attractive but requires more water.

*"Punctata" means dotted
(in this case, leaves,
stems and calyx).*

Illustration by
Marie Orlin

Garden in late spring

Spring

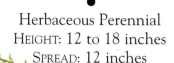

Linum perenne var. lewisii

LY-num pe-REN-nee
Blue Flax, Lewis' Flax, Prairie Flax, Perennial Flax
Linaceae—Flax family

❖

Herbaceous Perennial
HEIGHT: 12 to 18 inches
SPREAD: 12 inches

Illustration by
Marjorie C. Leggitt

*New flowers
form each day.*

LANDSCAPE USE
Attractive singly or in groups in informal gardens. Very attractive in shortgrass, mid-grass or tall-grass meadows. Blue flax is short-lived, but self-seeds generously, so is best planted where you can enjoy it moving about from year to year.

FORM
Erect, airy, vase-shaped.

NATIVE RANGE
Western Great Plains from Canada to Mexico. 9,500-foot elevation in Colorado.

CHARACTERISTICS
FLOWER: multitudes of dainty, 1-inch, sky-blue, five-petaled flowers open each morning, and fall by late afternoon. Blooms in late spring or early summer; frequently reblooms if cut back after initial flush of flowers.
LEAVES: alternate narrow 1-inch leaves on wiry, arching stems.

CULTURE
SOIL: prefers well drained, but tolerates clay.
EXPOSURE: full sun, part shade.
PROPAGATION: easy to grow from seed.
WATER: low to moderate.
HARDINESS ZONES: 2 to 8.
LIFE SPAN: short (3 to 4 years).

BEST FEATURES
Self-sows abundantly, filling spaces in naturalized areas with color for a long period.

COMPANION PLANTS
Eschscholzia californica (California Poppy), *Saponaria ocymoides* (Soapwort) and *Cerastium tomentosum* (Snow-in-summer).

DISADVANTAGES
Short-lived; turns brown and unsightly in late summer if not cut back; cannot be assigned a permanent location in formal perennial borders, because it invariably dies and self-seeds in a preferred locale.

SUBSPECIES OR VARIETIES
Linum perenne spp. *alpinum* is 2 to 12 inches tall with 3/4-inch flowers.

Early summer garden

Nepeta x faassenii

NE-pee-ta FAAS-sen-nee-eye
Catmint
Lamiaceae—Mint Family

Herbaceous Perennial
HEIGHT: 18 inches
SPREAD: 30 inches

LANDSCAPE USE
Excellent summertime ground cover. Good for front of dry border or rock garden.

FORM
Casually mounded.

NATIVE RANGE
Sterile hybrid of garden origin. Catmint originated in Europe and is now widely distributed in North America. Overwinters in Colorado at about 3,500 to 6,000 feet.

CHARACTERISTICS
FLOWER: profuse, long lasting spikes of lavender-blue flowers in early summer. Shear off spent flowers for late summer rebloom.
LEAVES: gray-green, fragrant foliage.
FRUIT: none.
STEMS: square.

CULTURE
SOIL: adaptable to any well drained soil.
EXPOSURE: full sun, light shade.
PROPAGATION: division or cuttings.
WATER: adapts to wet or dry conditions. Less water usually means a more erect plant.
HARDINESS ZONES: 4 to 8.
LIFE SPAN: long; fast growing.

BEST FEATURES
When this plant is in bloom, the flowers almost obscure the foliage. When out of bloom, the soft silvery foliage always appears cool and fresh. Does not become invasive via seeds because it is a sterile hybrid.

COMPANION PLANTS
Stachys lanata (Lamb's Ears), *Pinus mugo* (Mugo Pine) and Verbena *Asclepias tuberosa* (Butterfly Weed).

DISADVANTAGES
Susceptible to mites; attractive to cats.

RELATED SPECIES
N. cataria (Catnip)—lavender-white flowers, $2^1/_2$ feet, reseeds readily.
N. mussinii (Catmint)—low growing at $1^1/_2$ feet, reseeds readily.
N.f. 'Blue Wonder'—compact mounds of bright blue flowers.
N.f. 'Six Hills Giant'—large, somewhat sprawling form with lavender flowers.

Illustration by
Cynthia Cano

Cool flowers and fragrant foliage will grace any garden.

Oenothera missouriensis

ee-noh-THEE-rah mis-sur-ee-EN-sis
Ozark Sundrop, Missouri Evening Primrose
Onagraceae—Primrose Family

❖

Herbaceous Perennial
HEIGHT: 10 to 12 inches
SPREAD: 18 to 24 inches

Early-summer garden

Early-summer flower

LANDSCAPE USE
Weaves among other plants, nice rock-garden plant, dry prairie hillsides, part shade, summer ground cover.

FORM
Prostrate, trailing stems with tips growing upright. Soft, silky appearance.

NATIVE RANGE
Nebraska, Missouri and Texas. Can be established up to 8,000 feet in Colorado.

CHARACTERISTICS
FLOWER: large, lemon-yellow flowers open from red buds toward the end of the day. Flowers last until the next day. Flowers all summer.
LEAVES: 5 inches long, silky look, deep green.
FRUIT: winged capsule, 2 to 3 inches long and wide, excellent for dried wreaths.

CULTURE
SOIL: dry, sandy, can tolerate poor soils, good drainage.
EXPOSURE: full sun, part shade.
PROPAGATION: sow seeds anytime.
WATER: low.
HARDINESS ZONE: hardy to zone 4.

BEST FEATURES
Blooms through the "dog days" of summer. Deer resistant.

COMPANION PLANTS
Phacelia campanularia (Annual Desert Bluebell), *Bergenia cordifolia* (Heart-Leafed Bergenia) and *Perovskia atriplicifolia* (Russian sage).

RELATED SPECIES
O. caespitosa (Tufted Evening Primrose)—6 to 8 inches; nice native; loves clay soil; white flowers turn pink as they age. *O. speciosa* (Showy Evening Primrose)—6 to 8 inches. Pink flower stays in bloom all summer. *O. berlandieri* 'Siskiyou'—large white flowers with pink edges; hardier than *O. speciosa*.

Illustration by
Karen Boggs

O. caespitosa

O. missouriensis

Fall

Summer

Parthenocissus quinquefolia

par-then-o-SIS-us kin-ka-FOL-ea
Virginia Creeper, Woodbine
Vitaceae—Grape Family

❖

Deciduous Vine
HEIGHT: 9 inches as ground cover
SPREAD: 50 to 70 feet

Illustration by
Linda Evans

*Summer
leaf and
fall fruit
and leaf*

LANDSCAPE USE
Big, vigorous vine that clings or runs over fence, ground, trellis or brick wall. Can be grown through a small tree; beautiful growing among boulders; good ground cover on slopes.

FORM
Woody trunk and stems form a dense blanket of green foliage.

NATIVE RANGE
Southern New England, west to Ohio, Illinois, Missouri.

CHARACTERISTICS
FLOWER: insignificant.
LEAVES: 6 inches, 5-lobed, green leaves that turn orange to scarlet in the fall.
FRUIT: small grapelike fruit, which attracts birds, forms in late summer. Although related to grape, the berries and leaves are toxic to humans and should not be ingested.
STEMS: woody, sending out side tendrils, that cling to most surfaces.

CULTURE
SOIL: needs good depth of fertile soil to become established quickly, but will do well in most soils.
EXPOSURE: grows well in sun to filtered shade.
TOLERATES: drought, urban pollution and extreme cold.
PROPAGATION: cuttings establish easily.
WATER: very low.
HARDINESS ZONES: 3 to 9.
LIFE SPAN: long; growth rate medium to fast.

BEST FEATURES
Fast growing once established; beautiful fall color; can control erosion on banks; attractive to birds.

DISADVANTAGES
If planted against wood or shingle siding, it can be difficult to remove at repainting time.
Can develop severe powdery mildew if grown in shade. Can shade out plants by growing over them. Seeds spread easily.

SUBSPECIES OR VARIETIES
P. q. engelmannii (Engelmann's Ivy) has smaller leaves, denser growth and tendrils with adhesive disks. Related species—
P. tricuspidata (Boston Ivy) also grows on masonry buildings with adhesive tendrils; evergreen.

Late summer landscape

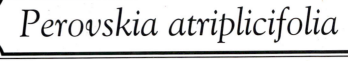

Perovskia atriplicifolia

Late summer color

pe-ROV-ski-a a-tri-pli-si-FOH-li-a
Russian Sage
Verbenaceae—Verbena Family

Subscrub Perennial
HEIGHT: 3 to 5 feet
SPREAD: 3 to 4 feet

Winter form

LANDSCAPE USE
Striking plant for the middle or back of border; useful as a hedge or screen; place in median strips or among other shrubs.

Perennial Plant Association's 1995 Plant of the Year.

FORM
Dense, compact, shrublike perennial resembling Salvia.

NATIVE RANGE
Central Asia including Iran, Afghanistan, Pakistan and Tibet. Will survive up to 8,000 feet in Colorado.

CHARACTERISTICS
FLOWER: small, lavender-blue flowers encircling branched spikes situated on top of rodlike, downy white stems in late summer.
LEAVES: finely cut, silvery gray leaves have a downy appearance. The foliage has a sagelike aroma and is sticky to touch, especially in winter. The smell is thought to discourage deer from browsing. In cold climates foliage may die back to ground level during winter.

CULTURE
SOIL: average soil with good drainage.
EXPOSURE: full sun.
PROPAGATION: seeds or cuttings from softwood.
WATER: low water is sufficient; too much water will cause the plant to grow quite large, resulting in a floppy appearance. Drought tolerant.
HARDINESS ZONES: 4 to 8.
LIFE SPAN: long.
NOTE: cutting the plant back to the ground each spring makes for a more compact plant and encourages heavier flower production.

BEST FEATURES
The blue flowers attract bees and butterflies and, in some places, praying mantises.

COMPANION PLANTS
Combines nicely with *Callirhoe involucrata* (Poppy Mallow), *Delosperma cooperi* (Purple Ice Plant) and *Echinacea* (Coneflower).

DISADVANTAGES
Winter kills easily if planted late in season or in wet winter conditions.

SUBSPECIES OR VARIETIES
'Blue Spire' is an upright form of Russian Sage growing to 3 feet and producing a large inflorescence.

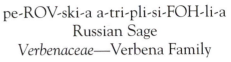

Illustration by Tana Pittman

107

Sunset Penstemon in early summer

PEN-ste-mon
Penstemon, Beardtongue
Scrophulariaceae—Snapdragon Family

Herbaceous Perennial
HEIGHT: 4 to 48 inches
SPREAD: 6 to 36 inches

Illustration by
Angela Overy

LANDSCAPE USE

The low, ground-cover varieties work well along pathways and among rocks. The taller varieties are appropriate in beds, mixed borders, among rocks, as a foreground to walls and fences and as spectacular specimen plants.

FORM

Habits range from mat-forming to tall, erect, multi-stemmed specimens. Over 200 species.

NATIVE RANGE

Primarily the western United States, to a lesser extent, the eastern United States. Most western varieties can be established up to 8,000- or 9,000-foot elevations.

CHARACTERISTICS

FLOWER: inflorescence generally one-sided; individual flowers are tubular or funnel-shaped, some more obviously than others; united corolla is 2-lipped, 2 lobes above and 3 below and not always distinctive; "Penstemon" comes from (pen=almost) and (stemon=stamen); colors vary among species (red, blue, purple or white).
LEAVES: the least distinguishing characteristic: although always opposite, they vary in color from gray to dark green and are variously shaped from narrow and grasslike to broad, oval or lance-shaped.

CULTURE

SOIL: prefers sandy or gravelly soil or will tolerate any soil that is well drained.
EXPOSURE: nearly all will succeed in full sun but will grow better in light shade planted in a hot climate.
PROPAGATION: sow seed in the fall or divide in the spring or fall. Some can be grown from cuttings.
WATER: some will do well on moist sites, most western prairie, foothill or desert species prefer dry conditions.
HARDINESS ZONES: 2 to 10.
LIFE SPAN: variable; usually short-lived (about 3 to 4 years). Longevity can be extended by not overwatering and cutting the seed heads off after bloom. Penstemons tend to reseed readily.

P. palmeri, P. 'Bridgesii', P. cu. 'Husker's Red', P. strictus and P. barbatus

Best Features
There is a large selection of species and cultivars, always with showy flowers and providing a variety of bloom times. Most tall species are attractive to hummingbirds.

Companion Plants
Associate with native ornamental grasses and shrubs.

Some Drought-hardy Species
P. ambiguus (Phlox or Sand Penstemon)—2 feet tall, round, airy clump of multiple stems and branches clustered with grasslike leaves. Comes alive in early to midsummer with phloxlike pinkish white or bright pink flowers. Native range is the dry sandy grasslands of Texas, New Mexico, Arizona, Colorado and Kansas. Good in zones 5 to 10. Must have good drainage.

P. barbatus (Scarlet Bugler Beardtongue)—2 to 4 foot tall flower spikes arise from a low mound of uncrowded, dark green basal leaves. Heavy bloom of narrow, bright scarlet, tubular flowers in early summer can be extended with deadheading until fall. Native to mountainous regions of Colorado, New Mexico, Utah and Arizona. Good in zones 2 to 7. Short-lived but self-sows readily. Several cultivars: 'Prairie Dusk'—rose-puple; 'Prairie Fire'—vermillion; 'Elfin Pink'— clear pink; 'Schooley's Yellow'—yellow.

P. caespitosus (Mat Penstemon)— 1 to 12 inches tall, carpetlike, compact mat of gray or green, narrow leaves spreading to 3 feet and covered with lavender-purple flowers from early to late spring. Native to sagebrush ecosystems of Utah, Colorado and Wyoming, generally in clay or rocky soils. Good in zones 4 to 8.

P. clutei (Sunset Penstemon)—1 to 4 inch mound of blue-gray foliage from which arise numerous 3-foot flower spikes supporting large sunset-pink flowers in early to midsummer with sporadic bloom until early fall. Evergreen foliage. Susceptible to root rot if soil isn't well drained. Short-lived. Native to Arizona in volcanic ash around 6,000 feet. Good in zones 4 to 8.

P. gracilis (Slender Penstemon)—10 to 20 inches tall, slender flower spikes surrounded with pale violet-blue flowers about 3/4 inch long during early to mid-summer. Light green leaves are finely toothed, with the basal ones more blunt than the longer ones, more pointed terminal leaves. Native to sandy or gravelly sites in southern Canadian and northern U.S. prairie states, south to Nebraska and eastern Colorado. Good in zones 3 to 6.

Others
P. eatoni, *P. cardinalis*, *P. strictus*, *P. pinifolius* and many more.

Sand Penstemon in summer

◀*Scarlet Bugler in early summer*

Mat Penstemon in spring

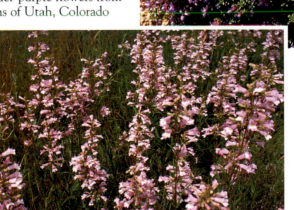

Slender Penstemon in summer

Polygonum aubertii

po-LIG-o-num aw-BER-te-i
Silver Lace Vine
Polygonaceae—Buckwheat Family

❖

Deciduous Vine
HEIGHT: 25 to 35 feet
SPREAD: as much as 10
to 15 feet in one season

Winter

Late-summer garden

LANDSCAPE USE
Good for a summer screen on fences and arbors, particularly in dry locations. Could be used as an informal ground cover. Ideal for covering a chain-link fence.

FORM
Intertwining mass of trailing, twisting stems.

NATIVE RANGE
Western China. Hardy to 9,000 feet in Colorado.

CHARACTERISTICS
FLOWER: very small, white, greenish white or pinkish, clustered into sprays covering the plant from mid to late summer.
LEAVES: bright green, heart-shaped and covering the whole plant. Fall color is not significant.
STEMS: in order to climb, it requires a structure such as a chain link fence or lattice to allow stems to wrap around.
ROOT: spreads by underground rhizomes.

CULTURE
SOIL: any well drained soil. Less rampant in clay soils.
EXPOSURE: full sun or part shade.
TOLERATES: dry alkaline soil.
PROPAGATION: stem cuttings, division, seeds, easily propagated.
WATER: tolerates wide range; easy to maintain with little water.
HARDINESS ZONES: 4 to 7; evergreen in 8 or 9.
LIFE SPAN: long.

BEST FEATURE
Showy flower display. Ideal for hot, dry sites. Nice foliage.

COMPANION PLANTS
Flowers about the same time as *Zauschneria arizonica* (Hummingbird Flower) and *Zinnia grandiflora* (Golden Paperflower).

DISADVANTAGES
May become weedy. Its above-ground growth can be controlled by cutting it back to the ground each winter.

Sprawling vine with cordate leaves and showy fall flowers

Illustration by
Cynthia Cano

110

Summer seed head

*Reddish purple
spring flower*

Blue flower in spring garden

Pulsatilla vulgaris

pul-sa-TIL-a vul-GAR-is
European Pasqueflower
Ranunculaceae—Buttercup or Crowfoot Family

❖

Herbaceous Perennial
HEIGHT: 9 to 12 inches
SPREAD: 6 to 10 inches

LANDSCAPE USE
Most often found in rock gardens; most effective in drifts.

FORM
Furry appearance. It is completely covered with hairs.

NATIVE RANGE
English chalk uplands and cold mountainous areas of the Northern Hemisphere. Can be established up to 9,500 feet in Colorado.

CHARACTERISTICS
FLOWER: reddish purple to blue, 2-inch flowers, with yellow centers often appear before leaves are fully developed. One of the earliest bloomers in the spring.
LEAVES: deeply cut, green and silky, forming a tuft at ground level.
FRUIT: the seed heads form a feathery plume that persists into the early part of the summer.

CULTURE
SOIL: neutral to alkaline. Requires excellent drainage, particularly in the winter.
EXPOSURE: full sun; tolerates partial shade.
PROPAGATION: sow in the garden as soon as the seed is ripe in early summer.
WATER: low to moderate.
HARDINESS ZONES: 4 to 8.
LIFE SPAN: long.

BEST FEATURES
Showy early spring flower with attractive seed heads.

COMPANION PLANTS
Rubus deliciosus (Boulder Rasberry), *Sempervivum* spp. (Hens and Chicks) and most all rock garden plants.

DISADVANTAGES
Skin irritation may occur when handling this plant.

CULTIVARS
P. vulgaris 'Rubra' (red flower). *P. vulgaris* 'Alba' (creamy white). *P. patensis* is native to the western United States.

Illustration by
Linda Evans

Expends energy blooming in the early spring when water is available

111

Ratibida columnifera

ra-ti-BID-a col-um-NI-fer-a
Prairie Coneflower, Mexican Hat
Asteraceae—Sunflower Family

Herbaceous Perennial
HEIGHT: 18 to 24 inches
SPREAD: 12 to 18 inches

Late-summer garden

LANDSCAPE USE
Naturalize in grassland planting, cutting garden, herbaceous flower beds.

FORM
Upright, freely branching from the base, airy clump.

NATIVE RANGE
British Columbia to New Mexico up to 8,000 feet.

CHARACTERISTICS
FLOWER: many slender stalks are capped by yellow to red, slightly drooping petals that surround an extended center, giving the flower the appearance of a sombrero.
LEAVES: bright green, finely divided, narrow and lacy.
ROOT: long taproot.

CULTURE
SOIL: clay to sandy, well drained. Tolerates poor soil.
EXPOSURE: sun.
PROPAGATION: seed; divide.
WATER: very little water required but will tolerate moist soil.
HARDINESS ZONES: 4 to 10.
LIFE SPAN: short (2 to 3 years); reseeds.

BEST FEATURES
Easy to establish, flowers first year and stays in flower most of the summer.

COMPANION PLANTS
Bouteloua gracilis (Blue Grama), *Buchloe dactyloides* (Buffalograss), *Ceratoides lanata* (Winterfat), *Gaillardia* spp. (Blanket Flower), *Penstemon* spp., *Liatris punctata* (Dotted Gay feather) and *Salvia officinalis* (Garden Sage).

DISADVANTAGES
Short-lived.

Easy to grow even in poor soil.

Illustration by
Angela Overy

Late-summer garden

SAL-vi-a of-fic-in-AL-is
Garden Sage
Lamiaceae—Mint Family

❖

Herbaceous Perennial
HEIGHT: 18 to 24 inches
SPREAD: 12 to 18 inches

LANDSCAPE USE
Perennial mixed borders, planted in mass is very showy, rock gardens,
in containers and as a summertime hedge. Sheared regularly for kitchen use.

FORM
Compact, leafy and shrublike.

NATIVE RANGE
South Europe to Turkey, Asia Minor. Can survive to 9,000 feet in Colorado.

CHARACTERISTICS
FLOWER: tall spikes of violet-blue flowers appear in late summer and last until frost.
LEAVES: oval, fuzzy, wrinkled, gray-green, 1 to 2 inches long. Aromatic leaves used
either fresh or dried as an herb for meat dishes. Often evergreen in mild winters.

CULTURE
SOIL: poor but well drained or dry clay.
EXPOSURE: full sun.
PROPAGATION: the species can be started by seed, cuttings and division.
The cultivars by division and cuttings.
WATER: low to moderate. Handles drought well once established.
HARDINESS ZONES: 4 to 10.
LIFE SPAN: the diameter of the plant
slowly expands each year; after 2 or 3 years
the center begins to die out. (It should then be divided.)

BEST FEATURES
Colorful, long-lasting flowers. Attractive culinary leaves.

COMPANION PLANTS
Chrysothamnus nauseosus (Rabbitbrush) and
Machaeranthera bigelovii (Purple Aster).
Any full-sun perennial.

CULTIVARS
'Tricolor'—variegated leaves with gray-green,
cream, purple, pink or red. 'Aurea'—gray-green
and gold variegated foliage, nonflowering. 'Purpurea'—
gray-green and purple leaves. 'Icterina'—yellow-green
leaves. None as hardy as S. *officinalis*.

Illustration by
D. Brown Tejada

S. o. 'Purpurea'

S. o. 'Icterina'

S. *officinalis*

113

Summer bloom in its native setting

STAN-lee-ya pin-NA-ta
Prince's Plume, Golden Prince's Plume, Desert Plume
Brassicaceae—Mustard Family

Perennial Subshrub
HEIGHT: 4 to 5 feet
SPREAD: 2 to 5 feet

LANDSCAPE USE
Naturalized setting, background to perennial bed, foundation planting where water must be held to a minimum, breaks up the monotony of a 6-foot wooden fence.

FORM
Woody base with a cluster of coarse leaves producing stout herbaceous stalks, terminating in racemes of spidery, yellow flowers.

NATIVE RANGE
Found in desert shrub communities, piñon pine or juniper woodlands in the Rocky Mountain region between 4,500 and 8,000 feet. Also established in southern California, northwest Nevada to Texas and as far east as Kansas and the Dakotas.

CHARACTERISTICS
FLOWER: golden yellow, borne on 1-foot racemes from late spring to mid-summer. Long stamens, pistils and narrow petals give it a feathery appearance.
LEAVES: handsome gray or pale green leaves are generally larger at the base and become shorter (about 4 inches) at the top and vary from pinnate to simple.
FRUIT: seeds are produced in long slender pods called "siliques."

CULTURE
SOIL: tolerates poor, dry soils, particularly those containing calcium. Often found in selenium-rich soils, absorbing the selenium which is poisonous to livestock.
EXPOSURE: full sun.
PROPAGATION: easy to start from seed. Sow anytime.
TOLERATES: heat, cold and drought.
WATER: low, only necessary during driest periods to keep plant appearance up.
HARDINESS ZONES: 4 to 7.
LIFE SPAN: long.

BEST FEATURES
Very drought tolerant; spectacular flower and attractive leaves.

COMPANION PLANTS
Ceratoides lanata (Winterfat) and *Perovskia atriplicifolia* (Russian Sage).

DISADVANTAGES
Requires excellent drainage in winter.

Extended anthers, protruding pistils and narrow petals give these flowers their "spidery" appearance.

Illustration by
Jill Sanders Buck

Late-summer garden

Early-summer flower

Tanacetum densum

(*Chrysanthemum densum*)
tan-a-SET-um DEN-sum
Partridge Feather
Asteraceae—Sunflower Family

❖

Evergreen Perennial
HEIGHT: 6 to 8 inches
SPREAD: 8 to 12 inches

LANDSCAPE USE
Useful in rock gardens, south-facing slopes, dry walls and banks where silvery white foliage is desired.

FORM
Low mound or mat forming.

NATIVE RANGE
Turkey, Greece. Good to 6,500 feet in Colorado.

CHARACTERISTICS
FLOWER: $1/4$ to $1/2$ inch, yellow, buttonlike in early summer. Aromatic.
LEAVES: finely cut, silvery white, downy; resembling delicately curled feathers.
STEMS: white, fuzzy, leafy.

CULTURE
SOIL: drier soils with good drainage, normal to poor soils.
EXPOSURE: sun.
PROPAGATION: division of clumps and cuttings.
WATER: dry.
HARDINESS ZONE: 5 to 10.
ROOTS: stems root when they touch soil.

BEST FEATURES
Great, silvery white ground cover that loves heat, drought and sun. Used as an insect repellant. No longer recommended as a cooking herb.

DISADVANTAGES
Can get out of bounds even without water, but easily sheared to keep in bounds.
Can easily rot with too much water.

Illustration by
Susan Rubin

*Leaves
resemble feathers.*

115

Autumn garden

zowsh-NER-e-a ar-i-ZONE-i-ca
Hummingbird Trumpet, Arizona Zauschneria
Onagraceae—Evening Primrose Family

Herbaceous Perennial
HEIGHT: 12 to 24 inches
SPREAD: 2 to 4 feet

LANDSCAPE USE

Attractive, airy foliage in shortgrass meadow or flower garden; bright red patch of flowers is focal point in the fall landscape.

FORM

Erect, upright, thin, narrow-leaved stems with many flowers along the stems, spreading into an airy, compact patch or colony.

NATIVE RANGE

Western United States, primarily California and Arizona. Grows below 6,000 feet in Colorado.

CHARACTERISTICS

FLOWER: bright scarlet, tubular trumpets distributed thickly along the top 12 inches of the stem. Appear in early fall and lasts to frost.
LEAVES: olive green or gray-green, narrow and silky.

CULTURE

SOIL: adaptable to a wide range of soil textures as long as it is well drained.
EXPOSURE: full sun. Needs warm or hot microclimate. In areas with a short growing season, treat as an annual.
TOLERATES: wind, dry soil, low humidity and heat.
PROPAGATION: sow seeds in the spring. Easy to start from cuttings.
WATER: 14 to 16 inches per year. Concentrate watering during the hot season of active growth.
HARDINESS ZONES: 5 to 8.
LIFE SPAN: long; moderately fast growth.

BEST FEATURES

One of few plants with a colorful, fall flower display. Little maintenance except for annual spring removal of dead foliage and stems. Disease free.

COMPANION PLANTS

Contrast with dark green foliage of Junipers, the silver foliage of such plants as *Ceratoides lanata* (Winterfat) or *Artemisia* spp. or the deep purple of *Machaeranthera bigelovii* (Purple Aster).

DISADVANTAGES

Readily reseeds, therefore is somewhat invasive. Will not establish if planted late in season.

RELATED SPECIES

Z. *californica* 'Alba'—similar to Z. *arizonica* but with white flowers. Z. *californica* 'Solidarity Pink'—pink flowers. Z. *garrettii*—longer blooming and shorter height.

Great hummingbird attraction in late fall

Illustration by
Sandie Howard

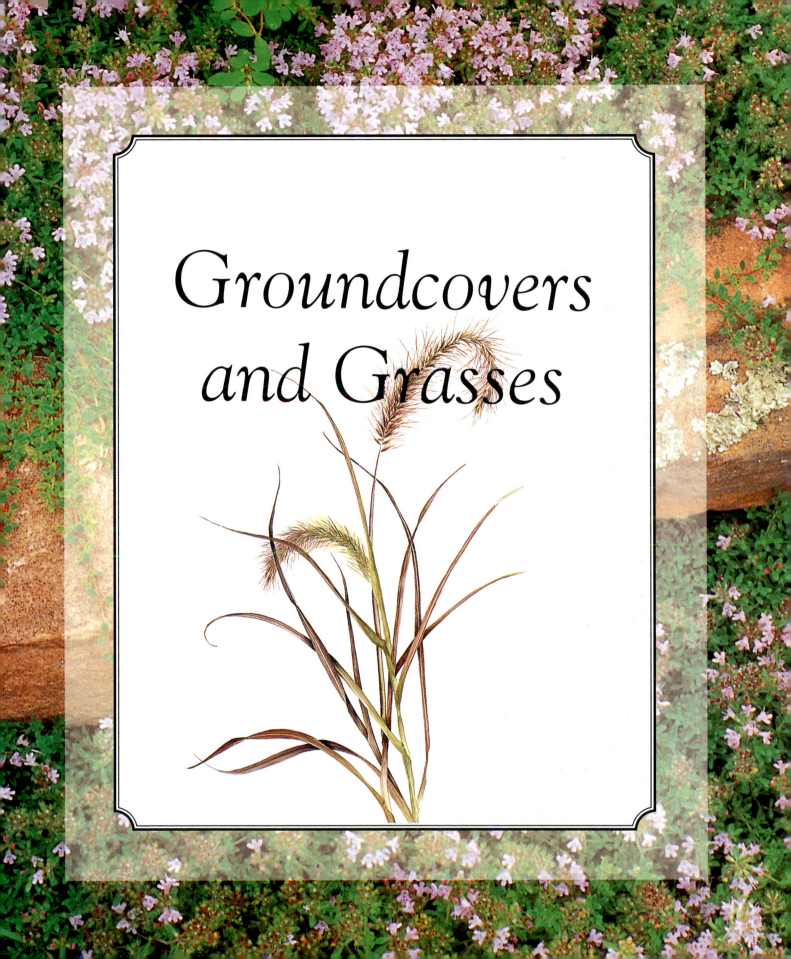

Groundcovers
and Grasses

Crested Wheatgrass lawn

Agropyron cristatum

ag-ro-PY-ron cris-TA-tum
Crested Wheatgrass
Poaceae—Grass Family

Perennial Bunch Grass (used as a turf)
HEIGHT: naturally 1 to 3 feet. Mow to 3 inches
SPREAD: 1 to 2 feet

LANDSCAPE USE
As an informal, mowed turf where aesthetics are not primary but soil stability, reduced watering, moderate foot traffic and low maintenance are important: outlying or minimally used areas of parks, road and utility right-of-ways, empty lots, extensive home backyards. Also serves well unmowed for erosion control, roadside stabilization. Seed heads are ornamental if left unmowed.

FORM
Cool season, medium bunch grass.

NATIVE RANGE
Introduced from Siberia through Canada and now widely spread throughout the semiarid western states as a forage and soil stabilization grass. Can be established up to 9,000 feet in Colorado.

CHARACTERISTICS
FLOWER: insignificant when mowed as a turf. Unmowed, are attractive: golden color in narrow spikes resembling wheat.
LEAVES: mostly basal, light green to blue-green, 1/4 to 3/8 inch wide.
ROOT: deep, 3 to 4 feet, finely branched and widespread.

CULTURE
SOIL: best on moderately deep, semi-fertile, silty loam to clay loam, not so good on sand. Will tolerate mild acidity, salinity and alkalinity.
EXPOSURE: sun to part shade.
TOLERATES: drought, cold and wind.
PROPAGATION: sow 5 pounds of seed per 1,000 square feet at a depth of about 1/2 inch. Sow in the spring or fall with adequate soil moisture available. Limited sod is available.
WATER: 10 to 15 inches annually. Requires supplemental water during the dry, hot, mid to late summer months to keep it green.
GROWING SEASON: "cool season" grass. Will stay green well past fall frosts and as soon as water is available and soil temperature is above freezing in the spring.
HARDINESS ZONES: 4 to 8.
LIFE SPAN: long.

BEST FEATURES
Good drought hardiness. Low fertility requirement. Works well as a mountain property lawn. Can be mixed with Smooth Brome and Western Wheatgrass in seed mix for lawn use, or used alone.

DISADVANTAGES
Tends to become semi-dormant during the hot, dry summer months without supplemental water. Additional water revives the green color. Requires reseeding, if physical damage occurs. Seeded heavily, it becomes a nice thick sod, although tends to "thin" a little as it matures, especially with repeated mowings. To maintain a thicker sod, mow to no less than 2¹/₂ or 3 inches.

CULTIVARS
Colorado State University turf trials reveal 'Hycrest' to be the most satisfactory as a turf. 'Ephrium' works fairly well, but forms a thinner turf more likely to suffer weed invasions. 'Fairway' and 'Ruff' are also good as turf.

Early-summer bloom

Summer garden

Pussytoes between flagstone

Antennaria rosea

an-te-NA-ri-a RO-ze-a
Pink Pussytoes, Meadow Pussytoes
Asteraceae—Sunflower Family

Perennial Ground Cover
HEIGHT: 4 to 12 inches
SPREAD: 8 to 12 inches

LANDSCAPE USE
Effective between paving stones in a walkway. Appropriate for rock or wildflower gardens.

FORM
Low carpet of leaves from which rise short, slender flower stalks.

NATIVE RANGE
From Alaska down through western Canada into the United States where it is established on the slopes of the foothill, mountain and alpine zones.

CHARACTERISTICS
FLOWER: blooms early in the summer. The blooms are clustered like the toes of a cat and predominately pink, but also is available in white and rose. The flower itself is $1/4$ inch long.
LEAVES: woolly, grayish green spoonlike leaves approximately 1 inch in length grow in a basal rosette.

CULTURE
SOIL: prefers sandy, well drained but will adapt to poor clay soils.
EXPOSURE: full sun.
PROPAGATION: seed or division.
WATER: extremely drought tolerant.
HARDINESS ZONES: 2 to 8.

BEST FEATURES
Makes nice dried flowers; grows under less than ideal conditions.

COMPANION PLANTS
Sempervivum spp. (Hen and Chicks) or *Sedum spurium* 'Dragon's Blood' (Dragon's Blood Stonecrop Sedum).

DISADVANTAGES
Plants self-sow and spread rapidly into surrounding areas. Under dry conditions, leaves may go dormant after flowering. To prevent dormancy, add a little extra water or keep flowers clipped.

SUBSPECIES OR VARIETIES
Antennaria parvifolia (Dwarf Pussytoes)—flower is white, native to Colorado.

Leaves grow close to the ground, protecting them from wind and reducing transpiration.

Illustration by
Susan Rubin

119

Sideoats Grama is pictured in the foreground of this garden.

◄ *Late summer*

BOO-te-loo-a cur-ti-PEND-u-la
Sideoats Grama Grass, Tall Grama Grass
Poaceae—Grass Family

❖

Warm Season Perennial Bunch Grass
HEIGHT: 1 to 2 feet
SPREAD: 1 foot

LANDSCAPE USE

Popular grass for meadows and reclamation. In the garden, it can stand alone as an accent or be planted with others along a walkway. A tall ground cover.

FORM

Tall, erect, stems rising above dense tufts of fine-textured leaves.

NATIVE RANGE

In the United States, widely distributed eastward from the Rocky Mountains to the Allegheny Mountains, and from north to south its range is from Montana to Arizona and Texas. Viable at 9,000 feet in Colorado.

CHARACTERISTICS

FLOWER: spikelets form on one side of the stem about midsummer. They emerge purplish and later develop bright orange anthers.
LEAVES: narrow, bluish green leaves dry to a brown color.
FRUIT: spikelets form seeds and drop off after maturity.
ROOT: short, scaly rhizomes tend to make this semi-sod-forming.

CULTURE

SOIL: adapted to a variety of soils from sandy to clay; least tolerant of loose sands and heavy clays. Tolerant of some salinity.
EXPOSURE: full sun; good winter hardiness.
PROPAGATION: easy to establish from seed if sown 2 months before the first fall frost.
WATER: drought tolerant; will do well on 12 to 16 inches per year.
HARDINESS ZONES: 4 to 8.

BEST FEATURES

Unusual flower and seed display along the stem; remarkably hardy under less-than ideal conditions. Invasiveness is very slow.

COMPANION PLANTS

B. curtipendula is a nice contrast to the dark greens and the broad leaves of *Callirhoe involucrata* (Wine Cups) or *Centranthus ruber* (Red Valerian). Excellent with *Gaillardia* or *Ratibida*.

CULTIVARS

'Butte' and 'Vaughn'.

RELATED SPECIES

B. gracilis—used as a turf grass, 8 to 10 inches tall, seed heads form "flags" at the end of the stems. Also makes a great ornamental clump grass.

Note the orange-red anthers in this late-summer grass.

Illustration by
D. Brown Tejada

Blue Grama lawn

Bouteloua gracilis

BOO-te-lou-a GRASS-il-is
Blue Grama Grass
Poaceae—Grass Family

❖

Turf Grass or Ornamental Clump Grass
HEIGHT: naturally 6 to 24 inches. Mow to 3 inches.
SPREAD: slowly by weak rhizomes, possibly 2 inches per year.

LANDSCAPE USE
As a ground cover or lawn on any sunny location not requiring any or very little supplemental irrigation: well groomed, home landscapes, untended, natural settings mixed with wildflowers, public right-of-ways and steep banks to control erosion.

FORM
Warm season, bunch grass, which becomes more sod-forming when mowed regularly.

NATIVE RANGE
Common throughout the Great Plains and arid foothills and mountain slopes of the southwest, up to 8,500 feet in Colorado. Due to short season, doesn't work well above 6,500 feet as turf. (State grass of Colorado.)

CHARACTERISTICS
FLOWER: unmowed, the inflorescence is made up of 1 to 3 "eyebrow"-shaped florets per stem (culm), usually at an angle, giving the plant its characteristic "flag" look. Flags (seed spikelets) persist into the winter and may have a slightly purple color.
LEAVES: narrow, fine textured, primarily basal, light green or gray-green, attractive tan during the fall and winter.
ROOT: deep, 3 to 4 feet and widespread.

CULTURE
SOIL: found in a wide range of soil types, from sandy to silty clay, but intolerant of pure sand or heaviest of clays. Tolerates poor soils, salinity and alkalinity.
EXPOSURE: full sun.
TOLERATES: cold and heat.
PROPAGATION: sow seed about 1/4-to 1/2-inch deep at a rate of 2 to 3-pounds per 1,000 square feet in the spring and up to at least 8 weeks before the first fall frost.
Blue Grama and Buffalograss seed are often mixed and planted together.
Also, at the time of publication, sod is available, but only as a mix of Buffalograss and Blue Grama.
WATER: low, 10 to 15 inches of natural and supplemental water per year is adequate to maintain an attractive turf.
GROWING SEASON: warm-season grass, does best during the hottest days of summer, especially when blessed with intermittent rain showers. Dormant between the first frost of fall and the last frost of spring.
HARDINESS ZONES: 4 to 8.
LIFE SPAN: long, slow spreading.

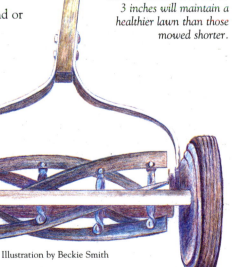
Mower blades set at 2¹/₂ to 3 inches will maintain a healthier lawn than those mowed shorter.

Illustration by Beckie Smith

BEST FEATURES
Low maintenance and low fertility needs. Attractive leaf color both summer and winter. Attractive, very ornamental seed heads if left unmowed. Relatively disease and pest free. Good as an erosion-control ground cover when left unmowed.

DISADVANTAGES
Short growing season. Intolerant of shade and high winter foot traffic. Seed cost is relatively high.

CULTIVARS
'Hachita', 'Alma' and 'Lovington' are fine as ornamental grasses (unmowed). 'Alma' and 'Hachita' have proved to do well as turf.

Buffalograss lawn

Buchloe dactyloides

BOO-klo dac-ta-LOY-deez
Buffalograss
Poaceae—Grass Family

Turf Grass
HEIGHT: naturally 4 to 8 inches.
Mow to 2¹/₂ or 3 inches or leave unmowed.
SPREAD: by stolons up to 12 inches per year

LANDSCAPE USE

Wherever an attractive, low-water, low-maintenance turf or ground cover is needed: home lawns, highway medians, steep hillsides, traffic islands, naturalized areas.

FORM

Low growing, warm season, sod forming, dense, smooth textured turf.

NATIVE RANGE

Shortgrass region of the central Great Plains, often mixed with *Bouteloua gracilis* (Blue Grama). Can be established as a turf up to the 6,500-foot elevation in Colorado.

CHARACTERISTICS

FLOWER: small spikelets; seed spikelets form at the base of the female plant while pollen is produced from spikelets situated on short stems (culms) at the top of the male plant.
LEAVES: blue or grayish green and narrow; fall and winter color is an attractive tan or reddish tan.
ROOT: widespread and deep, 3 or 4 feet (even in clay).

CULTURE

SOIL: usually found in silt or clay but will do fine in a wide range of types. Will require extra irrigation on sandy soils. Tolerates mildly alkaline soil.
EXPOSURE: full sun.
TOLERANT: regular mowing, heat and cold extremes.
PROPAGATION: sow the native Buffalograss, using "treated seed" 1/2 inch deep at a rate of 2 to 3 pounds per 1,000 square feet (Seed in nonirrigated areas in early spring or after first frost in the fall.) Seed or sod in irrigated areas between the last frost in spring and 8 weeks before the first expected fall frost. Seed will not germinate until soil temperatures warm. Sod can also be broken up to form plugs which can be spaced 1 foot apart and will, in a short time, fill in the spaces.
WATER: low, 10 to 15 inches annually of natural and supplemental water is sufficient to keep this grass looking nice.
GROWING SEASON: best during the heat of summer. Begins to green up in the spring after the last frost and go dormant after the first or second fall frost.
HARDINESS ZONES: 5 to 7.
LIFE SPAN: long, fast spreading.

BEST FEATURES

Very drought tolerant. Low maintenance because it can be left unmowed and has low fertilizer requirements. Attractive summer and winter color. Very little trouble from insects or disease. Can be established from seed, sod or plugs.

DISADVANTAGES

Shorter green season. Tends to thin out with excessive foot traffic, water, fertilization, shade and weeds. Cost of seed and sod is high. Slower to establish without any irrigation.

CULTIVARS

'609'—available only as sod—has an extended season of growth (well into October for Denver). More tolerant to shade and foot traffic. It consists of female plants only, with the seed heads at the base. In addition, turf trials at Colorado State University have given the following cultivars high ranking: 'Buffalawn', the 'Highlight' series and '315'.

▲ *Planted alone as a specimen*

Clustered together in a summer landscape ▼

Calamagrostis acutiflora

'Karl Foerster'
cal-a-ma-GROS-tis a-cute-i-FLOR-a
Karl Foerster Feather Reed Grass
Poaceae—Grass Family

Ornamental Bunch Grass
HEIGHT: 3 to 6 feet
SPREAD: 1 to 2 feet

LANDSCAPE USE
Let it stand alone as a specimen or in closely planted clusters such as in a low screen, temporary hedge or border planting, or as vertical accents in a perennial composition.

FORM
Cool season, upright and erect with many stems (culms) and leaves forming a dense clump.

NATIVE RANGE
Europe. Good to 7,500 feet in Colorado.

CHARACTERISTICS
FLOWER: in early summer inflorescence is open, feathery and purplish bronze; in late summer it is closed and has turned to a light tan color which persists into winter.
LEAVES: dark green, erect and standing about ¾ the height of the flower stems (culms).
ROOT: clumps will slowly enlarge with weak rhizomes.

CULTURE
SOIL: adaptable to any, even heavy, clay.
EXPOSURE: full sun. Tolerates some shade although culms are not as upright.
PROPAGATION: divide in the fall or spring.
WATER: prefers moist soils but is adaptable to drier conditions once established.
HARDINESS ZONES: 5 to 10.
LIFE SPAN: long.

BEST FEATURES
It is the most upright of all the ornamental grasses. Is attractive year-round. Excellent as a cut or dried plant. Few pests.

COMPANION PLANTS
The blue colors of *Festuca ovina glauca* (Blue Fescue), *Salvia officinalis* (Garden Sage) and Tulips. Tulips provide early color. Feather Reed Grass grows and hides old Tulip foliage as it turns brown.

DISADVANTAGES
If any, it is the minor maintenance required to keep it from looking uncluttered. Cut the plant back to near ground level in late winter as new grass leaves start to appear.

OTHER SPECIES
There are over 100 species of *Calamagrostis* native to Europe and North America. The cultivar 'Karl Foerster' is named after a European horticulturist who first recognized the ornamental value of grasses; it is sterile and will not re-seed.

Erect stems and inflorescence make an eye-catching feature in any Xeriscape.

Illustration by
Nancy Wilbur Nelson

123

Cerastium tomentosum

se-RAS-tea-um toe-men-TOE-sum
Snow-in-Summer
Caryophyllaceae—Pink Family

❖

Perennial Ground Cover
HEIGHT: 8 to 12 inches
SPREAD: 12 to 18 inches or more

Illustration by
Tanya McMurtry

*Thick mat of spreading stems and
narrow leaves help cool the soil and reduce evaporation.*

LANDSCAPE USE

A versatile ground cover that is at home in rock gardens, dry stone walls, as edging along paths or as a turf where there is not a lot of foot traffic.

FORM

Mat-forming perennial with a fine, soft texture.
To keep plant looking neat, shear after the flowers fade; can also be mowed.

NATIVE RANGE

Mountains of Italy. Can overwinter up to 7,500 feet in Colorado.

CHARACTERISTICS

FLOWER: white, 1-inch flowers bloom profusely in late spring and early summer.
LEAVES: 1-inch long, gray leaves are lance-shaped with a hint of green; have fine, soft texture.
FRUIT: capsules.

CULTURE

SOIL: grows well in sandy or clay soils, but should be well drained, spreads rapidly in moist, fertile soils.
EXPOSURE: full sun or part shade.
PROPAGATION: seed, division (spring or fall).
WATER: low to moderate.
HARDINESS ZONE: 5 to 9
LIFE SPAN: long.

BEST FEATURES

Beautiful display of white flowers in spring. The striking, gray foliage creates an element of surprise in the garden as well as conveys a sense of calm. It also harmonizes well with green foliage and the entire color spectrum.

COMPANION PLANTS

Mixes well with spring flowering perennials such as Iris, Atlas Daisy and Red Valerian.

DISADVANTAGES

Can be invasive; dividing plants can control spreading; susceptible to spider mites. May die out in center of plant if overwatered; requires shearing after bloom to keep plant compact, healthy and to prevent unwanted seedlings.

Spring garden

Fall

124

Note the characteristic
Ice Plant leaf blisters.

Illustration by
Angela Overy

Delosperma cooperi

del-o-SPERM-a COOP-er-i
Pink Hardy Ice Plant
Aizoaceae—Carpetweed Family

Perennial Ground Cover
HEIGHT: 6 inches
SPREAD: 24 inches

LANDSCAPE USE

Excellent ground cover that can be used alone, in rock gardens, as edging, on slopes to reduce erosion or to fill in around other plants.

FORM

Thick carpet of spreading stems.

NATIVE RANGE

South Africa. Can be established up to 6,000 feet in Colorado.

CHARACTERISTICS

Flower: hot pink, approximately 2 inches across; blooms from late spring to early fall with the showiest display in midsummer.
Leaves: succulent, grayish green, cylindrical in shape, about 2 to 3 inches long. Covered with tiny blisters, giving the appearance of ice crystals. After first frost, they begin to turn plum purple and stay that way throughout the winter.

CULTURE

SOIL: adaptable to any soil texture, even clay if well amended and well drained.
EXPOSURE: full sun.
PROPAGATION: easiest is the use of cuttings set in the ground and well watered until roots are established. Seeds profusely unless deadheaded.
TOLERATES: light shade for short periods.
WATER: low, particularly after it is established.
HARDINESS ZONES: 5 to 10.
LIFE SPAN: long; fast growing.

BEST FEATURES

Adapts well to dry, hot conditions. Long length of bloom. Rarely bothered by deer.

COMPANION PLANTS

Perovskia atriplicifolia (Russian Sage) and *Callirhoe involucrata* (Poppy Mallow). Any silver foliaged plant.

DISADVANTAGES

Rather bland, dormant leaves and stems predominate throughout the late fall and winter. Does not tolerate heavy snowpack or winter moisture. Best if planted where dry or exposed, September through March.

Midsummer landscape

*Late summer and
early fall appearance*

Winter color

125

Delosperma nubigenum

del-o-SPERM-a nu-bi-JEN-um
Hardy Yellow Iceplant
Aizoaceae—Carpetweed Family

Perennial, Evergreen Gound Cover
HEIGHT: 1 to 3 inches
SPREAD: 12 to 16 inches

Spring garden

◀ *Summer*

Winter color

LANDSCAPE USE
Rock gardens, borders, fills in around other plants, ground cover on steep slopes.

FORM
Low, dense, creeping mat of green, jelly beanlike leaves.

NATIVE RANGE
Southern Africa. Can be established up to 7,500 feet in Colorado.

CHARACTERISTICS
FLOWER: yellow, 3/4 inch, daisy-shaped, late spring blossom.
LEAVES: succulent, cylindrical, bright green, purplish cast in the fall and winter.

CULTURE
SOIL: somewhat sandy, well drained. Soil drainage is particularly important in the winter.
EXPOSURE: full sun, tolerates a very hot site.
PROPAGATION: press cuttings into soil surface.
WATER: low, water during extended hot periods.
HARDINESS ZONES: 4 to 10.
LIFE SPAN: has a tendency to spread, therefore has a long life.

BEST FEATURES
Fast spreader, very drought tolerant, seldom browsed by deer.

COMPANION PLANTS
Tiny spring bulbs.

DISADVANTAGES
Does not tolerate foot traffic or heavy winter snow or moisture.

Spring and summer stems, leaves and flower

Illustration by Angela Overy

126

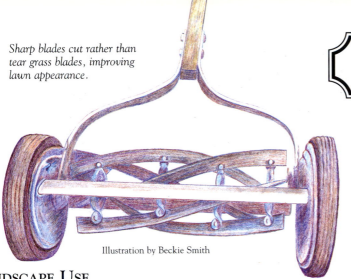

Sharp blades cut rather than tear grass blades, improving lawn appearance.

Illustration by Beckie Smith

Festuca arundinacea

fes-TU-ca a-run-din-A-cea
Tall Fescue
Poaceae—Grass Family

❖

Turf Grass
HEIGHT: naturally 1 to 3 feet. Mow to 3 inches
SPREAD: 1 to 2 feet

LANDSCAPE USE
Anywhere there is a need for a deep green turf and where water conservation is desired: home lawns, tree lawns between sidewalk and street, parks and recreation areas.

FORM
Cool-season, mid-sized bunch grass planted thickly to produce a turf.

NATIVE RANGE
Europe and planted widely throughout the United States as a pasture and a turf grass. Up to 9,000-foot elevations in Colorado.

CHARACTERISTICS
FLOWER: insignificant as a turf grass.
LEAVES: dark green, typically about 1/8 to 1/4 inch wide but narrower in some newer cultivars.
ROOT: large volume and mass, usually in the range of 3 to 4 feet deep in loose soil. Root mass acts to reduce compaction of soil, to cushion falls on sports fields and to draw upon moisture at deeper levels in soil. Tall Fescue is only drought tolerant if the soil is well amended and the extensive root system is allowed to develop.

CULTURE
SOIL: best on rich, silty clay but will do well on any well amended soil. Tolerates mild alkalinity, mild acidity, salinity and poor drainage.
EXPOSURE: full sun, filtered shade or part-day shade.
TOLERATES: extremes of heat and cold.
PROPAGATION OR ESTABLISHMENT: sow 6 to 8 pounds of seed per 1,000 square feet at a 1/4-inch depth. Sow in the spring in colder climates and late summer or early fall in warmer climates. (Late August through mid-September is best along the Colorado Front Range.) The other option is to transplant sod. To maintain vigor of this plant, mow no lower than 2½ inches and take off no more than 1/3 of the grass blade.
WATER: thrives on 30 inches per year but will do well on 18 inches of natural and supplemental water.
GROWING SEASON: cool-season grass. Most active growth is in spring and late summer or early fall. It begins greening before the last frost (usually before Bluegrass) and stays that way well past the first frosts of fall. In warmer climates it may remain green all year.
HARDINESS ZONES: 2 to 10.
LIFE SPAN: long.

BEST FEATURES
Deep root system, which gives it a large reservoir from which to draw water. The taller varieties hold up well under foot traffic. Not invasive to flower beds. Good disease and insect resistance. Does not form thatch like stoloniferous grasses. Needs less fertilization than Bluegrass. Good shade tolerance. Good for mountain area lawns.

DISADVANTAGES
Divots or physical damage to the turf must be reseeded or resodded for quick repair. It won't quickly self-heal like stoloniferous grasses such as Buffalograss or Bluegrass.

CULTIVARS
Dwarf varieties require less mowing than the original *F. arundinacea* because they are slower growing. They also have a blade size similar to Kentucky Blue Grass. Examples are 'Bonsai', 'Crewcut', 'Rebel Jr'., 'SR8200', 'Silverado', 'El Dorado', and 'Short Stop'. They tolerate normal foot traffic but are not recommended for sports fields. Taller varieties, developed as turf will withstand the rigors of a sports field although they have a broader leaf and will have to be mowed more often. They include such cultivars as 'Rebel', 'Falcon', 'Houndog', 'Olympic', 'Mustang' and 'Jaguar'.

Blue and green varieties of Blue Fescue

Festuca ovina glauca

FES-TEW-ka o-VIN-na GLAW-ka
Blue Fescue
Poaceae—Grass Family

Ornamental Perennial Grass
HEIGHT: 12 inches
SPREAD: 12 inches

LANDSCAPE USE
Wherever the soft texture and mounded "hummock" shape can provide contrast against other foliage types; in such locations as flower bed borders or in rock gardens as an accent plant. Looks particularly attractive in geometric planting patterns.

FORM
Fine-textured, compact clumps; does not spread by stolons.

NATIVE RANGE
Over most of North America except in the southwestern portion. Grows best below 8,500 feet in Colorado.

CHARACTERISTICS
Flower: wheat-colored spikes in early summer.
Leaves: silvery blue, narrow blades; some varieties tend toward green.

CULTURE
SOIL: well drained.
EXPOSURE: full sun to light shade.
PROPAGATION: seed, division.
WATER: dry, but looks best with some supplemental irrigation.
HARDINESS ZONES: 4 to 9.
LIFE SPAN: if center dies out, divide and replant.

BEST FEATURES
Blue leaves in summer and tan seed heads in fall and winter.

COMPANION PLANTS
Penstemon caespitosa 'Claude Barr' (Claude Barr Penstemon) and *Achillea ageratifolia* (Greek Yarrow).

SUBSPECIES OR VARIETIES
'Elijah's Blue' and 'Sea Urchin' are both varieties selected for their very blue foliage and compact growth habit.

DISADVANTAGE
Will not rot out most easily under wet winter conditions.

Flower stems deteriorate, but leaves remain through the year.

Illustration by
Sandie Howard

128

▲ *Late-summer garden*

▼ *Fall*

Helictotrichon sempervirens

hel-lick-toe-TRY-kon sem-per-VI-renz
Blue Avena Grass, Blue Oat Grass
Poaceae—Grass Family

Ornamental Perennial Grass
HEIGHT: 2 to 4 feet in bloom
SPREAD: 3 feet

LANDSCAPE USE
Architectural interest when used singly or in small groups; provides texture in borders.

FORM
Arching, dense, upright clumps or hummocks, similar to Blue Fescue except larger.

NATIVE RANGE
From rocky hillsides, Europe (southeastern France, northwestern Italy, southwestern Alps). Can be established up to 8,500 feet in Colorado.

CHARACTERISTICS
FLOWER: 6-inch panicle rises above foliage in summer.
LEAVES: upright, narrow, blue-gray, evergreen except in hard winter.

CULTURE
SOIL: well drained, indifferent to pH.
EXPOSURE: sun; tolerates light shade, particularly if not overwatered.
PROPAGATION: seed or divide clumps with sharp shovel or spade.
WATER: moderate to high.
HARDINESS ZONES: 4 to 9.
LIFE SPAN: grows moderately fast.
SEASONAL MAINTENANCE: cut back hard in spring or "comb" out dead leaves.

BEST FEATURES
Provides winter interest. Has attractive foliage. Is a great landscape plant.

COMPANION PLANTS
Callirhoe involucrata (Wine Cup), *Echinacea purpurea* (Purple Coneflower) and *Artemisia* (Sage).

DISADVANTAGES
Overwatering causes leaves to lose bluish cast.

Illustration by
Diane Neadeau Zimmermann

Combination of inflorescence and blue leaves makes this a useful accent plant.

129

Miscanthus sinensis

mis-KAN-thus si-NEN-sis
Miscanthus Grass, Maiden Hair Grass, Eulalia, Chinese Silver Grass
Poaceae—Grass Family

Perennial Ornamental Grass
HEIGHT: 4 to 10 feet
SPREAD: 3 to 6 feet

*Flower plumes and tall arching leaves
provide beauty all year long.*

Illustration by
Pamela Hoffman

LANDSCAPE USE

Three-season accent, big borders, screen, in mass.

FORM

Fountainlike habit formed by a dense tuft of upright, arching leaves through which several flower stems emerge.

NATIVE RANGE

Eastern Asia. Can be established up to 6,000 feet in Colorado.

CHARACTERISTICS

FLOWER: creamy white to rust-bronze, 6 to 10 inches long, feathery, arising on stems just above the leafy base in late summer and persisting into winter as tan or whitish.
LEAVES: tall, slender, arching, thick, gray-green to dark green.

CULTURE

SOIL: average garden soil.
EXPOSURE: sun to light shade.
TOLERATES: wind.
PROPAGATION: divide in the spring.
WATER: some varieties use less than others (see Cultivars).
HARDINESS ZONES: 4 to 7.
LIFE SPAN: about 20 years.

BEST FEATURES

Good architectural form spring and summer, showy, fall flower plumes and eye-appealing, winter interest.

COMPANION PLANTS

Cotoneaster divaricatus (Spreading Cotoneaster) and *Polygonum affine* (Himalayan Border Jewel).

DISADVANTAGES

Difficult to transplant.

CULTIVARS

'Gracillimus'—6 to 8 feet; olive green; most drought tolerant; fine upright habit. 'Morning Lights'—4 to 5 feet; bright green leaves; rust-bronze flower plumes; moist to somewhat dry; 'Purpurescens'—3 to 4 feet, bright green leaves turning reddish in the fall; bronze seed heads; moist to somewhat dry.

Miscanthus grass in early-summer garden.

Summer

Fall

Winter

Late summer

Oryzopsis hymenoides

(Stipa hymenoides)
or-e-ZOP-sis hym-en-OY-deez
Indian Ricegrass
Poaceae—Grass Family

Ornamental Bunch Grass
HEIGHT: 1 to 2 feet
SPREAD: 2 to 3 feet

LANDSCAPE USE
An accent in borders, perennial beds, rock gardens. Attractive in a naturalistic setting such as meadows or rocky hillsides.

FORM
Cool season, open clump with upright stems (culms) supporting airy seed panicles.

NATIVE RANGE
Distributed widely throughout the arid and semiarid western United States. From Canada into Mexico and from the Rocky Mountains to the Pacific Coast. Up to 9,500 feet in Colorado.

CHARACTERISTICS
FLOWER: flowers and the seed heads are open, graceful panicles, 3 to 9 inches long, made up of multipaired branchlets, each ending in a spikelet. Appear in early summer, persisting through the winter.
LEAVES: narrow, nearly as long as the culms and densely tufted at the base. Medium green color early and through midsummer, turning to tan in late summer through winter.

CULTURE
SOIL: prefers coarse-textured soils but is adaptable to all types as long as they are well drained.
EXPOSURE: full sun.
TOLERATES: drought, heat.
PROPAGATION: sow seed in the fall or winter at a depth of about 1 inch. Seeds are difficult to start sometimes, so put several in place when sowing.
WATER: very low.
HARDINESS ZONES: 3 to 7.
LIFE SPAN: short. Must be reseeded every few years, although this will happen naturally if the site is favorable.

BEST FEATURES
Attractive through several seasons. Excellent for dried bouquets.

COMPANION PLANTS
Ceratoides lanata (Winter Fat) and *Liatris punctata* (Dotted Gayfeather).

An ornamental grass appropriate for very dry sites

Illustration by
Susan T. Fisher

132

Summer garden

pen-i-SEE-tum al-oh-pek-yur-O-y-deez
Fountain Grass, Chinese
Fountain Grass, Rose Fountain Grass
Poaceae—Grass Family

Winter

Ornamental Grass
HEIGHT: 2 to 3 feet
SPREAD: 2 to 3 feet

LANDSCAPE USE
Fall perennial borders, building foundations, attractive in mass or as a specimen.

FORM
Dense tuft of arching, narrow leaves form an upright mound from which arise the inflorescences on thin stems. A warm-season grass.

NATIVE RANGE
Open ground on the Asian and Australian steppes.

CHARACTERISTICS
FLOWER: graceful "foxtail" flowers appear from mid to late summer. Inflorescence is about 4 to 10 inches long, 1 to 3 inches wide, ranging from creamy white to light pink or tan. Good for cut or dried arrangements.
LEAVES: narrow, bright green, approximately 18 to 30 inches long. As the season progresses, yellow and brown streaks appear on the leaves. They gradually fade from almond to straw-colored as winter approaches. This can be very attractive in late autumn.
FRUIT: in mid-autumn the flower shatters, the seeds drop, leaving the flower stems standing throughout the winter.

CULTURE
SOIL: prefers loamy but tolerates most soils if well drained.
EXPOSURE: full sun but will tolerate light shade.
PROPAGATION: division or seed.
TOLERATES: wind and heat.
WATER: low to moderate.
HARDINESS ZONES: 5 to 9.

BEST FEATURES
Attractive nodding inflorescence and arching leaves throughout the seasons.

COMPANION PLANTS
Lavatera trimestris (Lavatera), *Sedum spectabile* 'Autumn Joy' and Petunias.

DISADVANTAGES
Spreads invasively in warmer winter areas. Generally not hardy in colder parts of the Rocky Mountain region but makes an attractive, fast maturing annual grass.

CULTIVARS
'Hameln'—dwarf variety, 12 to 25 inches tall, 12 to 18 inches wide. 'Moudry'—dwarf variety 20 to 35 inches wide, with contrasting black awns on the seedheads.

Illustration by
D. Brown Tejada

Delicate features of this plant contrast nicely with broader-leafed forbes.

Pennisetum setaceum 'Rubrum'

Summer garden

pen-i-SE-tum se-Ta-seum ROOB-rum
Purple Fountain Grass or Crimson Fountain Grass
Poaceae—Grass Family

Ornamental Grass
HEIGHT: 2 to 4 feet
SPREAD: 2 to 3 feet

LANDSCAPE USE
Striking accent along the garden border, mass displays,
dried flowers.

FORM
Arching habit; symmetrical mound;
soft, featherlike flower plumes.

NATIVE RANGE
Africa.

CHARACTERISTICS
FLOWER: 14-inch, reddish purple flower plumes appear in late
summer and last until the first hard frost.
Plants remain attractive even after frost-killed.
LEAVES: flat blades are burgundy to bronze in color.
FRUIT: seedless.

CULTURE
SOIL: any well drained soil.
EXPOSURE: prefers full sun but will tolerate light shade.
PROPAGATION: divisions in the fall can be overwintered indoors
and replanted in the spring.
WATER: low to moderate.
HARDINESS ZONES: 8 to 10 grown as a perennial, in colder zones the plant
is not hardy and is used as an annual.
LIFE SPAN: long-lived perennial in the appropriate zone.

BEST FEATURES
Nice contrast to other green or gray garden foliage; fast growing;
attractive in fresh or dried arrangements.

COMPANION PLANTS
Especially attractive when planted with silvery foliage plants such as *Ceratoides lanata*
(Winterfat), *Santolina chamaecyparissus* (Lavender Cotton) or *Artemisia cana*
(Silver Artemisia).

DISADVANTAGES
This is an annual grass in cold climates.

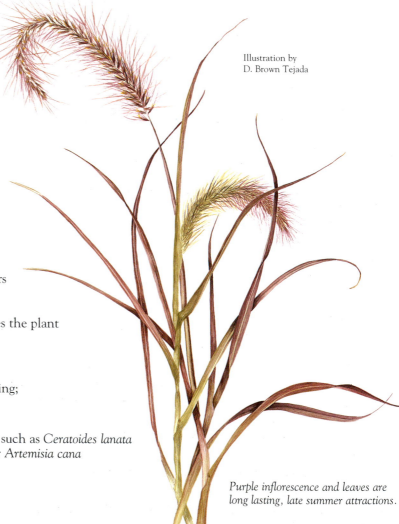

Illustration by
D. Brown Tejada

*Purple inflorescence and leaves are
long lasting, late summer attractions.*

Mid-summer garden ▼

▲ Fall

Santolina chamaecyparissus

san-toh-LI-nah kam-e-sip-ar-ISS-sus
Lavender Cotton
Asteraceae—Sunflower Family

Subshrub, Evergreen, Ground Cover
HEIGHT: 12 to 18 inches
SPREAD: 12 to 18 inches

LANDSCAPE USE
Rock gardens, knot gardens, lower desert landscapes, low hedge and carpet bedding.

FORM
Soft-textured mounds.

NATIVE RANGE
Mediterranean, southern Europe. Can be established up to 8,000 feet in Colorado.

CHARACTERISTICS
FLOWER: yellow, buttonlike, petalless flowers, 1/2- to 3/4-inch diameter, fragrant.
Many flowered heads during midsummer.
LEAVES: gray, compound, 1/2 to 1½ inches in length, which are finely divided into segments.
Musty fragrance.
FRUIT: achenes.

CULTURE
SOIL: dry, infertile, well drained.
EXPOSURE: full sun.
TOLERATES: heat, wind, alklaline soils.
PROPAGATION: cuttings in early summer; easy to start from seed.
WATER: drought tolerant.
HARDINESS ZONES: 4 to 8. May show dieback or complete loss along Front Range
in Colorado, especially in wetter soils.

BEST FEATURES
Woolly foliage persists through fall and winter. Plant is aromatic. Stem used as a moth
repellant. Deer resistant. Foliage color enhances colors of neaby plants.

COMPANION PLANTS
Iris spp. (Tall Bearded Iris) and *Penstemon* spp. (Penstemons).

DISADVANTAGES
May look untidy if not sheared annually after flowering.

RELATED SPECIES
Santolina virens (Green Lavender Cotton)—very similar growth habit, but has green leaves.
Not quite as hardy.

Illustration by
Melody Durrett

*Small woody basal stems
and summer flowers*

135

Polygonum affine

pol-IG-o-num a-FE-ne
Himalayan Fleeceflower
Polygonaceae—Buckwheat Family

❖

Perennial Ground Cover (semievergreen)
Height: 6 to 10 inches
Spread: 30 inches or more

Himalayan Fleeceflower adds year-round interest to the landscape.

Illustration by
Sandie Howard

136

LANDSCAPE USE
Borders, rock gardens, ground cover; good soil stabilizer on slopes.

FORM
Low, trailing mats, a medium texture in the landscape.

NATIVE RANGE
Asia and Japan. Good to 8,000 feet in Colorado.

CHARACTERISTICS
FLOWER: numerous spikes of rose-red or pink flowers stand out above foliage starting in late summer until frost, turning russet and persisting into winter.

LEAVES: bright green, narrow, mostly basal, turning copper-red in the fall and red into winter, particularly if exposed to the sun.

CULTURE
SOIL: adaptable to clay through sandy; tolerates poor soil.

EXPOSURE: sun to light shade.

PROPAGATION: division.

WATER: adaptable to moist or dry conditions; can get too aggressive with too much water.

HARDINESS ZONES: 4 to 10.

LIFE SPAN: short to moderate.

BEST FEATURES
Good fall color, low maintenance and tends to choke out weeds.

COMPANION PLANTS
Plant under light shade of *Gleditsia* spp. (Honey Locust) among *Prunus besseyi* (Western Sand Cherry) or in the foreground with ornamental grasses.

DISADVANTAGES
Needs some water in order to spread; grows weedy in rich soil.

OTHER SPECIES
'Border Jewel'—rose pink flowers.
'Darjeeling Red'—crimson pink flowers.
'Donald Lowndes'—bright pink.

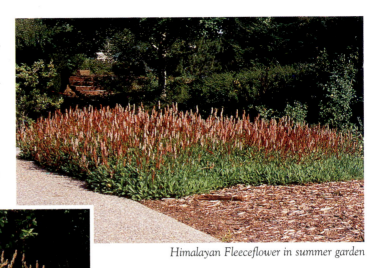

Himalayan Fleeceflower in summer garden

Summer

Spring

◄ *Fall*

Winter

Fall

Spring

Midsummer

Sedum spectabile

SEE-dum spec-TAB-il-ee
Showy Stonecrop, Live-forever
Crassulaceae—Stonecrop Family

❖

Succulent Perennial
HEIGHT: 18 to 24"
SPREAD: 10 to 15"

Illustration by
Lynn Janicki

▲ _Autumn Joy Sedum_

LANDSCAPE USE
Border, rock garden, attractive as a single specimen or in groups of 3 or more to form a tall ground cover or a small, summer hedge.

FORM
Upright clump, round growth habit.

NATIVE RANGE
Japan. Good to 8,000 feet in Colorado.

CHARACTERISTICS
FLOWER: large, flat heads of pink, red or white; blooming at the end of summer to frost.
LEAVES: smooth, egg-shaped, fleshy textured, blue-green leaves and paler, upright stems.
ROOT: thick and fleshy, forming a crown and doesn't spread.

CULTURE
SOIL: does best in sandy, poor to average quality, well drained. Does not tolerate poor winter drainage.
EXPOSURE: full sun or light shade.
PROPAGATION: divide clumps in spring, stem cuttings in summer.
WATER: moderate.
HARDINESS ZONES: 3 to 10.
LIFE SPAN: long.

BEST FEATURES
Showy, late summer flower. Easy to grow on difficult sites. Attracts many bees and butterflies.

COMPANION PLANTS
Salvia officinalis (Garden Sage), _Oryzopsis hymenoides_ (Indian Rice Grass) and _Zauschneria arizonica_ or _californica._

CULTIVARS
S. x 'Autumn Joy' (hybrid of _S. telephium_ and _S. spectabile_)—attractive year-round; grows best in poor soil and full sun; starts with masses of pink flowers in early summer, maturing to a salmon pink in late summer; in fall turns to rust red, fading to rust throughout the winter. 'Carmen'—rosy pink flowers. 'Brilliant'—reddish pink flowers. 'Meteor'—burgundy red flowers. 'Star Dust'—white flowers. 'Variegatum'—foliage green and yellow; pink flowers. 'Mohrchen'—purple-bronze foliage.

Parent plants with off-sets

Sempervivum species

sem-per-VI-vum
Hens, and Chicks, Houseleek
Crassulaceae—Stonecrop Family

❖

Creeping Evergreen Succulent
HEIGHT: 2 to 4 inches
SPREAD: 6 to 8 inches

Illustration by
Susan Rubin

LANDSCAPE USE
Container and dish gardens; very small spaces between rock retaining walls or slopes; rock garden in crevices of boulders; small landscape or garden—contrast with stone and fine-gravel paving.

FORM
Mat-forming, star-shaped, evergreen succulent rosette, spreading by roots and offsets around the parent plant.

NATIVE RANGE
High mountain areas of Europe, Morocco and West Asia. Can be established at elevations up to 8,000 feet in Colorado.

CHARACTERISTICS
FLOWER: star-shaped, small flower, white, yellowish, reddish or greenish, in clusters on top of 4- to 12-inch stalks depending on species. Stalk dies after flowering; nearby rosettes take its place. Midsummer flower period. No flower fragrance.
LEAVES: primary structure of the plant is made up of thick rosettes of succulent leaves.

CULTURE
SOIL: adaptable to any well drained soil; does best in gravelly and stony soil. No fertilizer needed.
EXPOSURE: full sun to light shade or part day shade.
PROPAGATION: very easy and fast from division of offset at base of center rosette.
WATER: 14 to 16 inches annually; supplement water during dry periods; less important when planted among stones where roots are covered and penetrated deeply into moist soil below.
HARDINESS ZONES: 4 to 10.
LIFE SPAN: very long; slow growing.

BEST FEATURES
Drought hardy. Great for tucking into rock wall pockets. Nice texture contrast with broadleaf plants.

COMPANION PLANTS
Best used alone, but can flourish under the dappled shade of such trees as *Gleditsia tri.intermis* (Thornless Honey Locust) or *Gymnocladus dioica* (Kentucky Coffee Tree).

DISADVANTAGES
Not tolerant of foot traffic. Difficult to weed if invaded by grasses, weeds or sedums.

OTHER SPECIES
At least 500 varieties and 40 species. *S. arachnoideum* (Cobweb Houseleek)—leaves joined by fine, white hairs; red flower; seldom blooms. *S. tectorum* (Hens and Chicks)—various flower colors, with stems to 2 feet tall.

Spring

◀ *Hens and Chicks in mid-summer bloom*

Summer

Delicate leaves and flowers of summer

Illustration by
Marilyn Taylor

Thymus pseudolanuginosus

TY-mus sue-doh-la-new-gi-NOH-sus
Woolly Thyme
Lamiaceae—Mint Family

Mat-forming Perennial Ground Cover
HEIGHT: 1 to 2 inches
SPREAD: 18 inches

LANDSCAPE USE
A low ground cover for rock gardens, herb gardens, between stepping stones or as an edging. Will tolerate some foot traffic. This thyme is ornamental rather than culinary.

FORM
Creeping habit, which forms a soft, undulating mat. It continues to root as it spreads.

NATIVE RANGE
Native to the Mediterranean. Appropriate for 8,500-foot elevations in Colorado.

CHARACTERISTICS
FLOWER: sprinkled with small, pink flowers in the early summer.
LEAVES: the gray-green leaves and stems are covered with dense, gray hairs, giving it a woolly appearance. Has a purple cast during the winter. A fragrant odor is emitted when the leaves are crushed.

CULTURE
SOIL: performs well in dry, alkaline, well drained soils; too much fertilizer or rich soils make the stems grow too tall and weak.
EXPOSURE: full sun or dry shade.
PROPAGATION: easy to grow from seed, division or cuttings.
WATER: low to moderate; very drought tolerant.
HARDINESS ZONES: 4 to 10.

BEST FEATURES
Needs very little supplemental water; spreads quickly and is aromatic.

COMPANION PLANTS
Can be used with other Thymes.

DISADVANTAGES
Occasionally suffers from root rot if overwatered or in poorly drained soil.

RELATED SPECIES
T. serpyllum (Mother of Thyme)—soft pink, rose or lavender flowers, scented leaves. *T.* x *citriodorus* is Lemon Thyme, a small evergreen shrublet with lemon scented leaves and lavender flowers.

Summer flower

Summer

Winter

140

Veronica with Pink Verbena, Yellow Evening Primrose and White Yarrow in midsummer.

Ver-ON-ik-a pek-ti-NAY-ta
Blue Woolly Speedwell
Scrophulariaceae—Figwort Family

Late summer

Spring

LANDSCAPE USE
Exceptionally attractive ground cover for full sun or light shade. Especially nice between stepping stones or where allowed to cascade over a wall.

FORM
Ground-hugging mat.

NATIVE RANGE
Asia Minor. Can be established to 8,500 feet in Colorado.

CHARACTERISTICS
FLOWER: profuse, tiny, cup-shaped, deep violet-blue flowers with white centers, in mid-spring on short 4-inch spikes. Sporadic bloom the rest of the year, with a few flowers braving the winter months.
LEAVES: dark green, wedge-shaped, furry with scallop-toothed edges, forming an attractive dense mat. Viewed from a distance, when out of bloom, it resembles a ground-hugging Juniper.

CULTURE
SOIL: any soil with reasonable drainage.
EXPOSURE: sun or part shade.
PROPAGATION: division.
WATER: low with an occasional deep soaking.
HARDINESS ZONES: 4 to 8.
LIFE SPAN: long.

Leaves as well as flowers are attributes of this plant.

BEST FEATURES
Attractive year-round; spreads freely; dense enough to discourage weeds; somewhat everblooming with dainty, blue flowers that complement most any companions.

COMPANION PLANTS
Wonderful underplanting for late red Tulips; exceptional with *Verbena canadensis* (Canadian Verbena) and *Oenothera missouriensis* (Ozark Sundrop).

Illustration by
Susan Rubin

DISADVANTAGES
Spent flower spikes require removal to keep it attractive. A weed whip or lawn mower works in the right location. Susceptible to slug damage. Spreading tendency can be checked by trimming the edges once or twice a year.

RELATED SPECIES
V. liwanensis (Turkish Veronica)—breathtaking cobalt blue, little or no rebloom, dense, less aggressive, spent flower spikes disappear on their own. *V. cinerea*—blue flower, silvery leaves, good soil drainage required. *V. pectinata* 'Rosea'—with pink flowers is probably even more common than the ones with blue flowers.

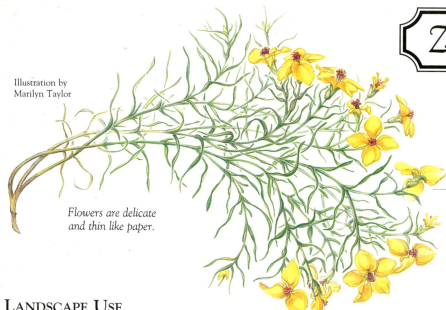

Illustration by
Marilyn Taylor

*Flowers are delicate
and thin like paper.*

Zinnia grandiflora

ZIN-i-a gran-di-FLO-ra
Paper Flower, Desert Zinnia,
Rocky Mountain Zinnia
Asteraceae—Sunflower Family

❖

Ground Cover or Subshrub
HEIGHT: 6 to 8 inches
SPREAD: 10 inches or more

LANDSCAPE USE
Effective when allowed to develop into large patches.
Use for dense ground cover, low borders and shortgrass meadows.

FORM
Lacy, compact mound.

NATIVE RANGE
Texas and Oklahoma panhandles, Colorado, New Mexico, Mexico, from 4,000 to 6,000 feet. Roadsides, dry mesas, hills and plains.

CHARACTERISTICS
FLOWER: bright yellow with orange anthers, 1 inch, daisylike,
covers plant from midsummer to early fall.
LEAVES: pale green, needlelike, densely produced.
FRUIT: seeds attached to rays of flowers.

CULTURE
SOIL: dry, calcareous, well drained.
EXPOSURE: sun.
PROPAGATION: seed from ray florets only, low germination rate.
Direct sow in early May, germination at 70° to 80° F. Root prune
by cutting around plants for a few years to thicken stand more quickly.
WATER: very low, will not tolerate moderate water. Water young
plants to encourage spread, then, once established, only needs 6
to 8 inches water per year.
HARDINESS ZONES: 4 to 7.
LIFE SPAN: short (2 to 3 years), but colonizes quickly.

BEST FEATURES
Very effective mass of low yellow flowers from June until frost.
Deer resistant. Very drought tolerant.

COMPANION PLANTS
Combines well with *Verbena* spp., *Artemisia* spp. *Echinacea purpurea*
(Purple Coneflowers) and clumps of *Festuca glauca* (Blue Fescue
Grass). Useful with Buffalograss in prairie lawns.

DISADVANTAGES
Need to be careful about plant getting too much water.
Poor performance in unamended clay soils. Hard to transplant.
Spreads quickly in sandy soils.

Midsummer

Late-summer garden

Annuals

Dry summer garden

Coreopsis tinctoria

cor-e-OP-sis tinc-TOR-e-a
Tickseed, Calliopsis, Golden Coreopsis
Asteraceae—Sunflower Family

Half-hardy Annual
HEIGHT: 18 to 40 inches
SPREAD: 4 to 8 inches

Illustration by
Ann Lowdermilk

LANDSCAPE USE
Brightens up dry problem areas with an abundance of sunny blooms. Good for naturalizing and is appropriate in more formal settings such as borders, edging and mixed annual-perennial beds.

FORM
Wispy stems support large flowers. When planted in mass, are very attractive and easily swayed by the wind.

NATIVE RANGE
Throughout the United States and Canada and particularly prevalent in the plains states and provinces.

CHARACTERISTICS
FLOWER: sunflower-shaped, about 1 inch across, variously colored: yellow, orange, purple, bicolored with reddish or purple-brown centers. Will last all summer if spent flowers are removed regularly.
LEAVES: medium green, narrow, growing at the base and along the stem.

CULTURE
SOIL: prefers light sandy but grows easily in any poor but well drained soil. Low fertilizer requirements.
EXPOSURE: full sun.
PROPAGATION: sow in the spring, barely cover seed.
WATER: very low to moderate.
LIFE SPAN: one season (annual).

BEST FEATURES
Bright, cheerful colors. Easy to grow. Good as a cut flower. Looks best when planted close together in mass.

COMPANION PLANTS
For color contrast use the annuals: *Cosmos bipinnatus* (Cosmos) and *Centaurea cyanus* (Bachelor's Button). Great for prairie gardens.

DISADVANTAGES
Can be blown over in a high wind or heavy rain.

Easy to grow under adverse conditions

144

Eighteen-to 48-inch plants bloom throughout the later part of summer.

Late-summer border

Cosmos bipinnatus

COZ-mos bi-pin-A-tus
Cosmos, Mexican Aster
Asteraceae—Sunflower Family

❖

Tender Annual
HEIGHT: 2 to 4 feet
SPREAD: single, wiry stem will have leaves and stems that spread approximately 6 to 12 inches

C. sulphureus

C. bipinnatus

Illustration by Karen Boggs

LANDSCAPE USE
Sunny flower beds and cottage gardens, meadows (perennial grasses will crowd Cosmos out after several years), open areas of a lawn.

FORM
Tall, open and branching, airy texture.

NATIVE RANGE
Tropical America and Mexico.

CHARACTERISTICS
FLOWER: cherry, white to rose pink 2- to 4-inch daisies with yellow centers appear on long wispy stems from midsummer to frost.
LEAVES: bright green, fine, deeply divided leaves give a lacy effect.

CULTURE
SOIL: well drained, poor soil (rich garden soil yields lush foliage but few flowers).
EXPOSURE: full sun, avoid windy locations.
PROPAGATION: seed outside after last frost.
WATER: low.
HARDINESS ZONES: all zones, during frost-free period.
LIFE SPAN: dies at first frost.

BEST FEATURES
Self-sows and grows with virtually no care, beautifying difficult areas that have dry, poor soil. Seeds on spent flowers attract birds. Flowers attract butterflies. Excellent cut flower.

COMPANION PLANTS
Native Sunflowers (*Helianthus annuus)* and Hollyhocks (*Alcea rosea*) are similar in height and enjoy the same conditions. Shorter flowers for a foreground might include *Salvia farinacea*, California Poppy and Alyssum. Marigolds and Zinnias would further enliven the mixture but would require some additional water to stay healthy.

DISADVANTAGES
Gets leggy; tall varieties require staking; susceptible to powdery mildew when grown in very dry locations; can self-sow excessively.

CULTIVARS AND OTHER SPECIES
C. bipinnatus is available in numerous named cultivars, varying in color from white to deep pink: 'Sea Shells' has unique fluted flower petals; 'Sonata Dwarf' is only 24 inches tall with strong stems; 'Candy Stripe' flowers are white and crimson. *C. sulphureus* (Yellow Cosmos [see illustration]) is 12 to 48 inches tall with fiery orange-red and golden yellow flowers; a broader leaf.

145

Its bright orange color is refreshing on dry, untended sites.

Eschscholzia californica

esh-SHOLT-zi-a kal-if-FORN-ik-a
California Poppy
Papaveraceae—Poppy Family

Hardy Annual or Short-lived Perennial
HEIGHT: 12 inches
SPREAD: 12 inches

LANDSCAPE USE
Good for naturalizing in wild gardens, also useful in beds, borders and containers.

FORM
Casually rounded.

NATIVE RANGE
Western United States.

CHARACTERISTICS
FLOWER: intense, bright orange, from spring to fall; blooms best in cool weather.
LEAVES: finely divided, blue-green foliage.

CULTURE
SOIL: adaptable but best in sandy or well drained.
EXPOSURE: full sun, light shade.
PROPAGATION: sow in fall or early spring. Watering well will aide germination.
WATER: once established in the spring, minimum water needed beyond natural precipitation.
HARDINESS ZONES: all, very hardy; fall emerged rosettes will survive to −30°F.
LIFE SPAN: usually one season. Some plants may overwinter along the Front Range in Colorado.

BEST FEATURES
Bright cheerful flowers that are easy to grow even in poor, dry soils.

COMPANION PLANTS
Penstemon strictus (Rocky Mountain Penstemon) and *Arctotis stoechadifolia* (African Daisy).

DISADVANTAGES
May self-sow excessively in rich, well watered soils. When self-sows, often new plants are different flower color of red, white, etc.

CULTIVARS
Many. 'Alba' (cream white), 'Rosea' (salmon pink)
'Thai Silk'—deep jewel tones and 'Mission Bells' (double, many colors) are some.

Planted close together, these plants make a colorful ground cover throughout the summer.

Illustration by
Tanya McMurtry

Summer garden

gom-FREE-na glob-O-sa
Globe Amaranth
Amaranthaceae—Amaranth Family

❖

Tender Annual
HEIGHT: 10 to 20 inches
SPREAD: 10 to 20 inches

Illustration by
Tana Pittman

LANDSCAPE USE
Containers, borders and beddings.

FORM
Dense mat of leaves from which rise erect, long, slender flower stems.

NATIVE RANGE
Far Eastern tropics.

CHARACTERISTICS
FLOWER: small, 1 inch, round, papery flower heads resembling clover.
Colors are purple, red, pink, lavender, white, orange and yellow
(depending upon cultivar).
LEAVES: green, oblong, opposite with slightly hairy margins, 1 to 2 inches long.

CULTURE
SOIL: light, sandy, poor and well drained.
EXPOSURE: full sun.
TOLERATES: heat, wind, humidity and drought.
PROPAGATION: start seeds indoors 6 to 8 weeks prior to last frost for earliest
bloom, otherwise, outdoors after last frost.
WATER: requires little water once established.
LIFE SPAN: one growing season (annual).

BEST FEATURES
Showy flower under adverse conditions. Makes excellent, long lasting cut or dried
flowers if they are cut before stems elongate.

COMPANION PLANTS
Arctotis stoechadifolia (White African Daisy) and *Ipomea* spp. (Blue Morning Glory Vine).

CULTIVARS
'Buddy', 'Strawberry Fields' and many more.

*Purple is only one color of
the many colors available.*

147

Lavatera
and Purple
Fountain
Grass

Late-summer garden

Lavatera trimestris

la-vah-TEH-ra tri-MEH-stris
Annual Mallow
Malvaceae—Mallow Family

Hardy Annual
HEIGHT: 2 to 4 feet
SPREAD: space 18 to 24 inches apart

Illustration by
Linda Evans

LANDSCAPE USE
Middle or rear of sunny, mixed border; colorful, fast growing, low, summer hedge.

FORM
Dense, bushy mound.

NATIVE RANGE
Southern Europe, Mediterranean region.

CHARACTERISTICS
FLOWER: satiny, 4-inch, hibiscuslike blooms in pink or white completely cover plant from mid-summer to frost.
LEAVES: large, attractive, medium green maplelike leaves.

CULTURE
SOIL: enjoys loamy, rich soil but tolerant of poor soils.
EXPOSURE: full sun.
PROPAGATION: sow seeds outdoors in very early spring or indoors February through March.
WATER: low to moderate.
LIFE SPAN: one growing season (annual).

BEST FEATURES
Eye-catching flowers; little care; fairly wind tolerant; great cut flower.

COMPANION PLANTS
Petunias, Tithonia and perennials.

DISADVANTAGES
Bloom begins late for an annual.

CULTIVARS
'Pink Beauty'—pale pink. 'Loveliness'—bright, deep rose pink; veins are deep carmine. 'Silver Cup'—salmon-rose with dark rose veins. 'Sunset'—deep rose. 'Mont Blanc'—pure white. 'Ruby Regis'—large cerise-pink, highlighted by darker veins.

An easy-to-grow
annual with
spectacular, late-
summer flower
display

148

Summer flowers

Portulaca grandiflora

por-tew-LAK-a gran-di-FLO-ra
Moss Rose, Rose Moss, Portulaca
Portulacaceae—Purslane Family

Tender Annual, Ground Cover
HEIGHT: 4 to 6 inches
SPREAD: 10 inches

LANDSCAPE USE
Best used in hot, dry, sunny areas. Good for rock gardens, edging, dry slopes, containers and between rocks in walls and open spaces between stepping stones.

FORM
Low growing, trailing succulent.

NATIVE RANGE
Brazil.

CHARACTERISTICS
FLOWER: notched, oval flower occurring terminally on trailing stem. Single and double blossoms, 1 to 2 inches, open in sunlight and close at night throughout the summer. Blossom colors are red, white, yellow and orange.
LEAVES: 1 inch long, spoon or oval shaped, simple, scattered, fleshy and greenish red.
FRUIT: small numerous capsules.
STEM: soft, fleshy and reddish.

CULTURE
SOIL: well drained, sandy and gravelly.
EXPOSURE: full sun.
PROPAGATION: sow seeds directly where the plant is to grow, best when temperature does not fall below 70°F.
WATER: dry.
HARDINESS ZONE: cold tolerant to 20° to 10°F; tolerates high temperatures.
LIFE SPAN: One season annual.

BEST FEATURE
A colorful, low growing, spreading plant that blooms all summer in hot, dry, sunny locations.

COMPANION PLANTS
Oenothera missouriensis (Ozark Sundrops) and *Anacyclus depressus* (Atlas Daisy).

DISADVANTAGES
Easily self-sows and is somewhat toxic to sheep.

CULTIVARS
Many, some single blossoms and others with double. 'Sundance', 'Sunglo'.

Illustration by
Karen Boggs

*Appropriate for a
hot, south-facing exposure*

Midsummer garden

Salvia sclarea

SAL-vi-a SCLA-ree-a
Clary Sage
Lamiaceae—Mint Family

Biennial Herb
HEIGHT: 3 feet
SPREAD: 1 to 2 feet

LANDSCAPE USE
Splendid background for lower growing annuals and perennials. Use in mixed borders or clustered together for a large display. Appropriate for the herb garden, too.

FORM
Herbaceous, large rosette of basal leaves with rigid spikes of showy flowers above.

NATIVE RANGE
Europe, Asia Minor and Central Asia. Good to 7,500 feet in Colorado.

CHARACTERISTICS
FLOWER: bluish white and complemented by the showy, pink bracts and calyces which extend the period of color after the flowers have faded. Flowering peaks around midsummer and is appealing into late summer.
LEAVES: broadly oval, hairy, gray-green, highly textured and have an aroma considered objectionable by some. Basal leaves are the largest and shrink in size toward the blossom.
FRUIT: readily self-sows.
STEMS: square.

CULTURE
SOIL: prefers light, dry, alkaline and well drained.
EXPOSURE: full sun to partial shade.
PROPAGATION: seed in the spring after the danger of frost or start from cuttings.
WATER: low, with occasional water during the hottest and driest parts of the summer.
HARDINESS ZONES: 4 to 7.
LIFE SPAN: 2 years; the first year a whorl of leaves is formed near the ground; the second year the stalk grows to produce the inflorescence.

BEST FEATURES
Showy flower and rich leaves. Lovely cut flower.

COMPANION PLANTS
Ephedra spp. (Mormon Tea) and *Echinacea purpurea* (Purple Cone Flower).

DISADVANTAGES
Heavy self-sower; odor of foliage.

OTHER SPECIES
S. sclarea var. *turkestanica*—tends to be a short-lived perennial.

Illustration by
D. Brown Tejad

The combination of flowers, bracts and calyces produces a spectacular inflorescence.

Summer close-up

Summer garden

Sanvitalia procumbens

san-vi-TAL-ee-a pro-CUM-bens
Creeping Zinnia
Asteraceae—Sunflower Family

Half-hardy Annual
HEIGHT: 4 to 6 inches
SPREAD: trails 12 to 16 inches
(space 4 to 6 inches apart)

LANDSCAPE USE
Edging, bedding, ground cover, rock gardens, walls, hanging baskets and steep banks.

FORM
Trailing, spreading mats.

NATIVE RANGE
Arid mesas of Mexico.

CHARACTERISTICS
FLOWER: small (1/2 to 1 inch), bright, single, golden yellow daisies with comparatively large, purple-black centers. Free-flowering midsummer through frost.
LEAVES: oval leaves form lush, deep green foliage.

CULTURE
SOIL: prefers well drained, light sandy soil, but will tolerate alkaline clay. (Avoid fertilization.)
EXPOSURE: prefers sun, but will tolerate light shade.
PROPAGATION: sow directly after all danger of frost (does not transplant well).
Rake lightly at planting.
TOLERATES: heat, drought.
WATER: low (once established); avoid overhead watering.
LIFE SPAN: one season (annual).

BEST FEATURES
Easy to grow in hot, dry, difficult areas; will grow thick enough to inhibit weeds; makes a neat, crisp edging along front of border or along a path; plants are self-cleaning; becoming popular for hanging baskets.

COMPANION PLANTS
Cosmos bipinnatus (Cosmos) or *Rudbeckia hirta* (Gloriosa Daisy).

CULTIVARS
'Flore Pleno'—double form. 'Mandarin Orange'—intense vivid orange, All America winner. 'Golden Carpet'—tiny, golden orange, single flowers with black centers. 'Yellow Carpet'— lemon yellow with black centers.

Dense thicket of stems and foilage inhibit evaporation from the soil.

Illustration by Ann Lowdermilk

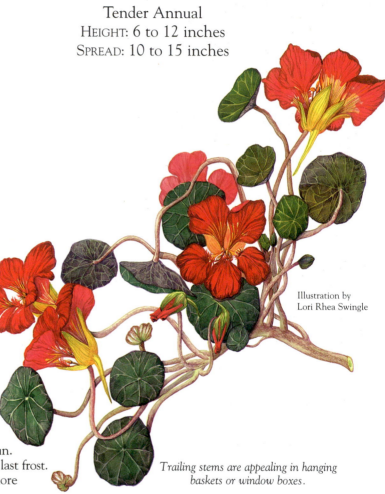

Tropaeolum majus 'Alaska'

tro-pe-O-lum MA-jus
Nasturtium
Tropaeolaceae—Nasturtium Family

❖

Tender Annual
HEIGHT: 6 to 12 inches
SPREAD: 10 to 15 inches

Nasturtiums are ideal high-altitude annuals.

Illustration by
Lori Rhea Swingle

*Trailing stems are appealing in hanging
baskets or window boxes.*

LANDSCAPE USE
Beds, hanging over walls, containers, hanging baskets.

FORM
Dense, compact and bushy.

NATIVE RANGE
Originally from the South American Andes.

CHARACTERISTICS
FLOWER: yellow, orange, mahogany and red. Supported on herbaceous stems rising above the leaves. Fragrant.
LEAVES: green, round with the stem connected to the center and veins radiating out from the connection.

CULTURE
SOIL: prefers sandy, infertile and well drained.
EXPOSURE: will not tolerate intense sun, heat or humidity. Plant in locations of dappled shade or morning sun. At cooler elevations (above 6,500 feet in Colorado), plant in all-day sun.
PROPAGATION: buy packaged seeds. Plant in the spring after the last frost.
WATER: prefers ample moisture in sandy soil and dry in the more clayish soils. Is drought tolerant.
LIFE SPAN: one season (annual).

BEST FEATURES
Attractive leaves and flowers all summer. Easy to grow. Edible flowers and leaves used in salads (similar to Watercress). Reported to be attractive to hummingbirds.

COMPANION PLANTS
Plant in mass as a show of its own, or plant in afternoon shade of taller shrubs such as *Potentilla fruticosa* (Potentilla) among tall perennials such as *Salvia officinalis* (Garden Sage) or with short grass varieties.

DISADVANTAGES
Susceptible to aphids and mealybugs.

OTHER SPECIES
Many older varieties tend to have a trailing habit; these are useful on trellises or fences.

Summer garden

ZIN-i-ah an-gus-te-FOH-li-ah
Narrowleaf Zinnia
Asteraceae—Sunflower Family

Annual
HEIGHT: 12 to 18 inches
SPREAD: 12 to 18 inches

Illustration by
Angela Overy

LANDSCAPE USE
Containers, window boxes, beds, borders, summer ground cover.

FORM
Trailing stems form a compact mound.

NATIVE RANGE
Mexico.

CHARACTERISTICS
FLOWER: profuse $1^{1}/_{3}$ inch, single, golden daisies, bloom all summer.
LEAVES: dark green and narrow.

CULTURE
SOIL: any well drained soil including that of low fertility.
EXPOSURE: full sun, plenty of air circulation.
PROPAGATION: sow seed in spring after soil warms.
WATER: moderate to dry.
LIFE SPAN: One annual season.

BEST FEATURE
Easy, carefree flower that is ideal for the casual, wildflower garden, attracts butterflies.

COMPANION PLANTS
Cynoglossum amabile (Chinese Forget-me-not) and *Helictotrichon sempervirens* (Blue Avena Grass).

DISADVANTAGES
Mildew may develop if leaves are regularly moistened during watering.

CULTIVARS
'Golden Orange' and 'Tropic Snow'.

Flowers bloom in orange, yellow and recently a white variety as well.

153

Shade Plants

Early-summer garden

Alchemilla mollis

AL-ke-mil-a MOL-lis
Lady's Mantle
Rosaceae—Rose Family

Herbaceous Perennial
HEIGHT: 12 to 18 inches
SPREAD: 12 to 15 inches

LANDSCAPE USE
Excellent as a ground cover under lightly branched shrubs, appropriate for perennial flower garden.

FORM
Broad mound of large, scalloped leaves, sprinkled with chartreuse open-flower clusters.

NATIVE RANGE
Caucasus and eastern Carpathian Mountains, Turkey. Can be established up to 7,000-foot elevations in Colorado.

CHARACTERISTICS
FLOWER: yellow-green to chartreuse in late spring, early summer.
LEAVES: round foliage with ruffled, scalloped margins; feltlike texture, grayish green.
FRUIT: not ornamental.

CULTURE
SOIL: adaptable, but in all cases, well drained.
EXPOSURE: dappled sun or partial shade.
PROPAGATION: seeds, division.
WATER: moist to somewhat dry.
HARDINESS ZONES: 4 to 10.
LIFE SPAN: long.

BEST FEATURES
Grayish green foliage, especially with morning dew or water globules on the leaves.

COMPANION PLANTS
Heuchera spp. (Coralbells), *Helianthemum mutabile* (Sun Roses), silver-leaved perennials. Excellent to help combine various colors in the flower border.

DISADVANTAGES
Needs more moisture when grown in full sun, otherwise, is susceptible to leaf scorch. Prone to spider mites, cut back midsummer to renew growth and beauty.

Illustration by
Susan Rubin

This large, coarse-textured plant is a nice contrast to small, many-flowered plants such as Woolly Veronica or Mat Penstemon.

Spring flower

Arctostaphylos uva-ursi

ark-to-STAFF-i-los you-va-UR-si
Kinnikinnick, Bearberry
Ericaceae—Heath Family

Broadleaf Evergreen Shrub
HEIGHT: 3 to 6 inches
SPREAD: 24 to 36 inches

LANDSCAPE USE
Evergreen ground cover particularly in rocky sites; wildlife gardens; naturalizing under trees or in rock gardens.

FORM
Prostrate, trailing, mat-forming.

NATIVE RANGE
North America, northern Europe and northern Asia, throughout the Rocky Mountains in gravelly, rocky sites up to 10,000-foot elevations.

CHARACTERISTICS
FLOWER: small, white, urn-shaped flowers tinged with pink; blooms in early spring.
LEAVES: dark, glossy green, firm texture.
FRUIT: scarlet red, rounded berry in the fall; attractive to wildlife.
BARK: peeling mahogany brown.

CULTURE
SOIL: prefers sandy, loamy or gravelly soil; needs good drainage; best in acidic soils.
EXPOSURE: shade to partial shade; doesn't do well in intense heat.
PROPAGATION: slow to germinate but can sow seed in the fall; use layering or stem cuttings. Best purchased from nursery.
WATER: dry to moist soils.
HARDINESS ZONES: 3 to 7.
LIFE SPAN: long.

BEST FEATURES
Year-round glossy evergreen foliage. Shade tolerant.

COMPANION PLANTS
Combines well with *Juniperus communis* (Common Juniper), *Pinus ponderosa* (Ponderosa Pine) and *Mahonia repens* (Creeping Grape Holly).

DISADVANTAGES
Intolerant of heavy clay soil that remains wet.

CULTIVARS
'Point Reyes'—pink flowers, rounder foliage. 'Alaska', 'Massachusetts' and other cultivars are available.

Illustration by
Nancy Wilbur Nelson

*One of only a few plants able to
grow in the shade of pine trees*

Bergenia cordifolia

ber-GEN-i-a cor-di-FO-le-a
Heartleaf Bergenia, Heartleaf Saxifrage
Saxifragaceae—Saxifrage Family

❖

Herbaceous Perennial
HEIGHT: 12 inches
SPREAD: 12 to 15 inches

Spring garden

Illustration by
Harriet Olds

LANDSCAPE USE
Mass grouping as ground cover, perennial flower garden.

FORM
Wide, rounded mound.

NATIVE RANGE
Siberia, Mongolia. Can be established up to 8,000 feet
in Colorado.

CHARACTERISTICS
FLOWER: pink to white flowers on stalks immediately above foliage; early spring.
LEAVES: large, oval, bold, glossy, dark green and thick-textured, up to 12
inches long. Turn red in the fall.
FRUIT: not ornamental.

CULTURE
SOIL: adaptable, but best in soils with added organic matter.
EXPOSURE: partial to full shade.
PROPAGATION: seed and division.
WATER: moist to somewhat dry.
HARDINESS ZONES: 4 to 9.
LIFE SPAN: long.

BEST FEATURES
Bold, glossy foliage; in mass makes
excellent border plant or ground cover.
Good red fall color.

COMPANION PLANTS
Heuchera sanguinea (Coralbells) or *Alchemilla mollis*
(Lady's Mantle).

DISADVANTAGES
Foliage may scorch spots especially if grown too dry.

CULTIVARS
'Perfecta'—20 inches tall with rose pink flowers;
'Evening Glow','Bressingham White',
Sunningdale' and several others.

*Once established,
this large herb will take moderately dry soil.*

Spring

Brunnera macrophylla

(Formerly *Anchusa myosotidiflora*)
BRUN-er-a mac-ro-PHIL-a
Perennial Forget-me-not, Siberian Bugloss
Boraginaceae—Borage Family

❖

Herbaceous Perennial
HEIGHT: 18 to 24 inches
SPREAD: 12 to 18 inches

LANDSCAPE USE
Partly shaded areas of the garden under open trees or among shrubs. Effective as a ground cover, specimen or in a border.

FORM
Strong clumps of large, basal leaves, above which hover tiny, bright blue flowers.

NATIVE RANGE
Eastern Mediterranean and western Siberia. Good to 9,000-foot elevations in Colorado.

CHARACTERISTICS
FLOWER: sky blue with yellow centers appear suspended in airy clusters above dark green leaves in late spring. Similar in appearance to annual Forget-me-not.
LEAVES: heart-shaped with obvious veination. Leaves become larger after the flowers fade, roughly 6 to 8 inches wide, making a nice ground cover.

CULTURE
SOIL: prefers finer textured, enriched soils such as clays or silts but is adaptable to a wide range.
EXPOSURE: prefers filtered shade, will tolerate full shade and morning sun.
PROPAGATION: sow seeds or divide clumps in the fall.
WATER: does well with plenty of water but is adaptable to dry conditions once established.
HARDINESS ZONES: 4 to 10.
LIFE SPAN: long.

BEST FEATURES
Attractive leaves and distinctive flowers.

COMPANION PLANTS
Plant among spring-flowering trees and shrubs such as *Kolkwitzia amabilis* (Beauty Bush) or *Caragana arborescens* (Siberian Pea Shrub) or with *Pulsatilla vulgaris* (Pasque Flower) and Tulips (red, orange).

DISADVANTAGES
Is susceptible to slug damage if the soil is kept damp.

CULTIVARS
'Variegata'—white leaf margins. 'Langtrees'—silvery white speckles at the margins. 'Hadspen Cream'—creamy white margins.

Illustration by
Nancy Wilbur Nelson

Fresh, sky blue flowers above broad foliage

159

Calamintha grandiflora

KAL-ah-min-thah GRAN-di-flor-a
Beautiful Mint
Lamiaceae—Mint Family

Herbaceous Perennial
HEIGHT: 12 to 24 inches
SPREAD: 10 to 15 inches

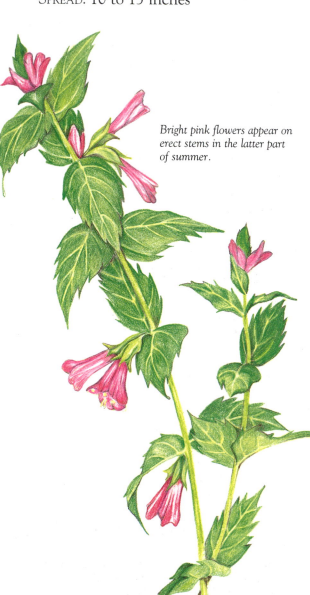

Bright pink flowers appear on erect stems in the latter part of summer.

LANDSCAPE USE
For the front of the border in lightly shaded areas or in containers.

FORM
Erect, bushy.

NATIVE RANGE
Southern Europe. Good to 6,000 feet in Colorado.

CHARACTERISTICS
FLOWER: long lasting, bright pink, tubular flowers cover the plant from midsummer to early fall.
LEAVES: pale green, toothed, opposite, aromatic.

CULTURE
SOIL: adaptable to any well drained soil.
EXPOSURE: full sun or filtered shade.
PROPAGATION: seed or division.
WATER: takes more water in full sun but will prefer it drier in light shade.
HARDINESS ZONES: 5 to 10. Best to mulch in zone 5 during the winter.

BEST FEATURES
Leaves and flowers have a pleasant, herbal fragrance. Long lasting bloom. Attracts bees, butterflies and hummingbirds.

COMPANION PLANTS
Heuchera spp. (Coralbells) in the shade or in the sun, and combine with an annual such as *Lobularia maritima* (Sweet Alyssum).

DISADVANTAGES
Won't survive severe drought. Stems are brittle.

Illustration by
Jayme S. Irvin

Campanula portenshlagiana

(*C. muralis*)
cam-PAN-u-la por-ten-SHLAG-ee-an-a
Dalmatian Bellflower
Campanulaceae—Bellflower Family

❖

Herbaceous Perennial
HEIGHT: 5 to 10 inches
SPREAD: 12 to 15 inches

*Long blooming,
blue, cuplike stars
above creeping
foliage*

Illustration by
Cynthia Cano

LANDSCAPE USE
Rock gardens, front of the border, containers, ground cover between shrubs or other plants.

FORM
Spreading, low mound.

NATIVE RANGE
Yugoslavia. Good to 9,000 feet in Colorado.

CHARACTERISTICS
FLOWER: broadly bell-shaped, face up, about 1 inch long, light purplish blue, free-flowering from mid-spring to late summer.
LEAVES: dark green, oval- to heart-shaped, margins deeply toothed and irregular; densely arrayed on procumbent stems.

CULTURE
SOIL: fertile, well drained garden soil, neutral to alkaline.
EXPOSURE: full sun in cooler climates above 7,000 feet or in zone 4. Light shade in warmer zones and at lower elevations.
PROPAGATION: sow seed in the spring for flowers the following spring or divide in the fall or early spring.
WATER: moderate to low once established.
HARDINESS ZONES: 4 to 10.
LIFE SPAN: long; divide every 2 to 3 years.

BEST FEATURES
Not invasive, although spreads moderately fast.
Long season of bloom.

COMPANION PLANTS
Calamintha grandiflora (Beautiful Mint) and *Rosa glauca*
(Red Leaf Shrub Rose).

DISADVANTAGES
Prefers more moisture during hot summer periods.

OTHER SPECIES
Other part shade, low water, low growing Bellflowers
include C. *rotundifolia* (Bells of Scotland),
C. *poscharskyana* (Siberian Bellflower)
and C. *carpatica* (Carpathian Bellflower).

Summer

This stoloniferous herb is an easy one to grow in dry shade.

Illustrations by
Marilyn A. Taylor

Galium odoratum

(*Asperula odorata*)
GA-li-um o-do-RA-tum
Sweet Woodruff, Bedstraw
Rubiaceae—Madder Family

❖

Herbaceous Perennial
HEIGHT: 6 to 8 inches
SPREAD: 15 inches or more, rhizomatous

Flowers are tiny but showy in mass.

LANDSCAPE USE
Mass grouping as ground cover, herb.

FORM
Low growing spreader with erect stems.

NATIVE RANGE
Europe, North Africa, Asia. Can establish up to 8,500 feet in Colorado.

CHARACTERISTICS
FLOWER: small white, star-shaped flowers on slender, erect stems producing a mass of white for several weeks in late spring.
LEAVES: small, bright green leaves encircle delicate, 4-angled stems. Pleasant, mild odor. Semievergreen.
FRUIT: not ornamental.

CULTURE
SOIL: adaptable to a wide range of soil types.
EXPOSURE: partial shade to full shade.
WATER: moist to somewhat dry.
HARDINESS ZONES: 4 to 10.
LIFE SPAN: long.

BEST FEATURES
Ability to grow under trees that provide dense shade.

COMPANION PLANTS
Best grown with shrubs or trees as a ground cover due to its spreading nature.

DISADVANTAGES
Can be invasive.

PROPAGATION
Division.

Spring flower

162

Sunny exposure in late spring

◄ *Flourishes in light shade*

Heuchera sanguinea

HEW-ker-a san-GWIN-e-a
Coralbells, Alum Root
Saxifragaceae—Saxifrage Family

❖

Herbaceous Perennial
HEIGHT: 12 to 18 inches
SPREAD: 12 to 15 inches

LANDSCAPE USE
Mass grouping as a tall ground cover, perennial flower garden, along garden path or in the dappled shade of a tree.

FORM
Dense clump of scalloped foliage topped with airy spikes of nodding flowers.

NATIVE RANGE
Hills and mountainous areas of New Mexico, Arizona and south to Mexico at elevations up to 9,000 feet.

CHARACTERISTICS
FLOWER: pink to white, bell-shaped flowers on slender stems several inches above foliage; blooms late spring through summer if spent flowers are removed.
LEAVES: rounded with shallow, lobed edges, mostly basal; generally rich green with marbling of silver.
FRUIT: not ornamental.
ROOT SYSTEM: shallow and fleshy, subject to frost heaving, which can be avoided by mulching.

CULTURE
SOIL: adaptable but prefers rich, well drained.
EXPOSURE: full sun to partial shade.
PROPAGATION: seed, division.
WATER: moist to somewhat dry.
HARDINESS ZONES: 4 to 10.
LIFE SPAN: long.

BEST FEATURES
Soft looking foliage, almost evergreen; delicate, airy, tidy appearance, not invasive. Old flower stalks are good in dried arrangements.

COMPANION PLANTS
In the shade—*Pulmonaria* spp. (Bethlehem Sage), *Brunnera macrophylla* (False Forget-me-not), *Anemone sylvestris* (Snowdrops Anemone); in the sun—*Hemerocallis* spp.(Daylily), *Campanula* spp. (Bellflower), *Veronica spicata* (Spike Speedwell).

DISADVANTAGES
None.

CULTIVARS
'Alba'—white flowers. 'Splendens'—scarlet red flowers. 'Chatterbox', 'Torch', 'June Bride' and many others.

Illustration by
Linda Lorraine Wolfe

Coralbells are adaptable to a wide range of environmental conditions.

Spring flowers

Lamium maculatum

LAY-me-um mac-u-LAT-um
Spotted Dead Nettle
Lamiaceae—Mint Family

Herbaceous Perennial
HEIGHT: 8 to 12 inches
SPREAD: 24 inches

LANDSCAPE USE
Under trees or the north side of structures. In borders, hanging baskets or as a tall ground cover.

FORM
Dense foliage forms on slender, spreading stems to produce a dense mat.

NATIVE RANGE
Europe and Asia. Good to 7,500 feet in Colorado.

CHARACTERISTICS
FLOWER: pink or purplish, 2-lipped flowers resembling Snapdragons. Early to late spring.
LEAVES: 2-toned, white in the center with dark green borders, heart-shaped or oval, semievergreen, opposite on the square stem typical of mint. About midsummer, cut back for renewed fresh growth for the fall.

CULTURE
SOIL: prefers rich soil but will do fine in any type or quality of soil.
EXPOSURE: partial shade or full sha
PROPAGATION: the species can be started from seed, cuttings and division. Cultivars, by cuttings and division.
WATER: high if available but is adaptable to dry conditions once established.
HARDINESS ZONES: 4 to 9
LIFE SPAN: long.

Two- lipped flower

BEST FEATURES
Delightful flowers and leaves. One of a few plants adaptable to dry shade.

COMPANION PLANTS
Brunnera macrophylla (Perennial Forget-me-not) and *Heuchera* spp. (Coralbells).

DISADVANTAGES
Somewhat invasive. Slugs like it.

CULTIVARS
'White Nancy'—Silver, white-centered leaves and white flowers, 6 to 12 inches tall, late spring to early summer. 'Beacon Silver'—wide, white center, pink flowers, requires shade, early to late spring. 'Pink Peuter' and 'Shell Pink' are other cultivars of note.

A variegated leafed plant that does surprisingly well in moderately dry shade

Illustration by
Libby Kyer

164

Mahonia repens

ma-HO-ne-a RE-pens
Creeping Grape Holly
Berberidaceae—Barberry Family

❖

Broadleaf Evergreen Ground Cover
HEIGHT: 1 to 2 feet
SPREAD: 6 feet

Summer fruit

Illustration by
Jill Sanders Buck

Spring flower

Fall garden

Spring

Summer

Winter

LANDSCAPE USE
Ground cover under shade trees, rock gardens.

FORM
Low spreading, coarse-textured.

NATIVE RANGE
Colorado mountain woodland areas,
up to 9,000 feet.

CHARACTERISTICS
FLOWER: yellow bloom in early spring. Fragrant.
LEAVES: shiny, dark green, hollylike leaves become mottled with red in the fall and completely bronze in the winter if exposed to the sun. Too much sun and wind during the winter will cause the leaf edges to burn.
FRUIT: small, edible, blue, grapelike fruits form in early summer and persist into winter.
BARK: gray or brown.
ROOT: spreads by underground stems.

CULTURE
SOIL: adaptable, but prefers loamy rich soil.
EXPOSURE: part to full shade.
PROPAGATION: sow seed in the fall.
WATER: adapts well to low water, though must be watered in dry winter periods.
HARDINESS ZONES: 4 to 7.
LIFE SPAN: moderate.

BEST FEATURES
Four-season appeal. Can be used in dry shade. Can be cut to 2 to 4 inches with mower if too tall. Will take 1 to 2 years to recover after mowing.

COMPANION PLANTS
Spring bulbs beneath trees.

DISADVANTAGES
Can get invasive if watered too much; slow to establish, winter burn.

RELATED SPECIES
M. trifoliata (Algerita)—8 feet tall, very drought tolerant. *M. haematocarpa* (Desert Holly)—12 feet tall, very cold-hardy. *M. aquifolium* (Oregon Grape Holly)—4 to 6 feet tall, sharply toothed leaves, dark bluish green in color.

Late spring garden

Philadelphus microphyllus

fil-ah-DEL-fus my-kroh-FIL-us
Littleleaf Mockorange
Saxifragaceae—Saxifrage Family

Deciduous Shrub
HEIGHT: 4 to 6 feet
SPREAD: 4 to 6 feet

Summer

Winter

Lack of disease and insect problems makes this an easy shrub to grow.

LANDSCAPE USE
This shrub is primarily of interest to native plant enthusiasts but has value wherever a small deciduous shrub is needed. May be used as a hedge or low screen. Splendid in perennial border and rock garden.

FORM
Upright, tight, compact and rounded.

NATIVE RANGE
Southwest United States; piñon juniper plant communities north to Wyoming, south to Mexico at elevations of 4,000 to 8,000 feet.

CHARACTERISTICS
FLOWER: solitary, 1-inch, snowy white flowers all summer; although these are widely reported to be fragrant, local populations are disappointingly lacking in this attribute.
LEAVES: 1¼ inches long, oval, dark green leaves, yellowish and not showy in fall.
FRUIT: odd, dry, prickly capsule.
BARK: reddish brown or tan; peels in narrow strips.

CULTURE
SOIL: any well drained soil.
EXPOSURE: sun to light shade.
PROPAGATION: seeds, cuttings or layering.
WATER: adaptable but best with occasional deep soaking.
HARDINESS ZONES: 4 to 10.
LIFE SPAN: long, slow growing.

BEST FEATURES
Tolerates neglect; some deer resistance.

COMPANION PLANTS
Calamintha grandiflora (Beautiful Mint) and *Rosa glauca* (Red Leaf Shrub Rose).

DISADVANTAGES
May become leggy. Prune for shape after flowering if desired.

OTHER SPECIES
P. lewisii (Lewis Mock Orange)—larger leaves and flower is more fragrant.

Illustration by
Janice Romine

Rosa glauca or Rosa rubrifolia

RO-za GLAW- ka or rueb-ri-FOL-i-a
Redleaf Rose
Rosaceae—Rose Family

❖

Deciduous Shrub
HEIGHT: 6 to 7 feet
SPREAD: 4 to 6 feet

Early summer garden

LANDSCAPE USE
Barrier plantings, background to perennial beds, mixed shrub borders, mixed perennial borders, and as specimen plants.

FORM
Upright, fairly open, arching branches, medium texture.

NATIVE RANGE
Mountains of central and southern Europe. Can be established up to 8,500 feet in elevation.

CHARACTERISTICS
FLOWER: single, light pink, emerging in early summer.
LEAVES: purplish in sun, grayish green in shade; pinnately compound. Excellent red-orange purple fall color.
FRUIT: large, dark red hips, oval shape.
STEMS: reddish bark, few thorns. Prune out old canes in the spring to keep it neat, and trim to control growth after flowering.

CULTURE
SOIL: adaptable to clay and sandy loams.
EXPOSURE: sun to partial shade.
PROPAGATION: cuttings or seeds.
WATER: moist to dry.
HARDINESS ZONES: 3 to 10.
LIFE SPAN: long.

BEST FEATURES
Attractive foliage, spring through fall, colorful hips in the winter and minimal thorns.

COMPANION PLANTS
Contrast leaves with *Shepherdia argentea* (Silver Buffaloberry) or *Stachys byzantina* (Lamb's Ears). Use *Bergenia, Brunnera* (False Forget-me-not) or *Pulmonaria* (Bethlehem Sage) in shade.

DISADVANTAGES
Single bloom season.

Simple, single flowers emerge in early summer; hips provide color in late summer and fall.

Illustrations by
Linda Evans

167

Ptelea trifoliata

TE-le-a tri-fo-li-A-ta
Hop Tree, Wafer Ash or Stinking Ash
Rutaceae—Rue Family

Large Shrub or Small Tree
HEIGHT: 15 to 20 feet
SPREAD: 15 to 20 feet

Illustration by
Susan Rubin

*Samaras appear in mid to late summer
and persist into winter.*

*Wafer Ash
in summer
landscape*

Early summer

Early-summer flower

LANDSCAPE USE
Hedge, specimen, ideal tree
for a small landscape.

FORM
A few strong leaders support open branching
and foliage, making a tall, rounded shrub, or if
pruned to one leader, an attractive, narrow,
small tree results.

NATIVE RANGE
Ontario and New York, south to Florida and west to Minnesota.
Can be established in Colorado from 4,500 to 9,000 feet.

CHARACTERISTICS
FLOWER: fragrant, greenish white clusters appear
in early summer.
LEAVES: glossy, dark green, alternate, trifoliate, oblong
leaflets 2 to 4 inches long.
FRUIT: compressed, broadly winged, circular samara.
BARK: dark gray, smooth with some warts.

CULTURE
SOIL: any texture type which is well drained.
EXPOSURE: full sun to heavy shade.
PROPAGATION: seed, cuttings or layering.
WATER: adaptable; native to moist woodlands
and dry, rocky uplands.
HARDINESS ZONES: 3 to 10.
LIFE SPAN: moderate.

BEST FEATURES
Good understory plant; adaptable to many conditions.
Not browsed by deer.

COMPANION PLANTS
Under a tall shade tree such as *Gymnocladus dioica* (Kentucky Coffee Tree)
or in association with *Rosa glauca* (Red Leaf Rose).

DISADVANTAGES
Tendency to sucker; bark and leaves emit strong aroma when bruised.

CULTIVARS AND RELATED SPECIES
'Aurea'—rich yellow, young leaves fade to lime green. 'Glauca'—blue-green leaves. *P.
angustifolia*—native to Colorado, New Mexico and Utah; similar features as *P. trifoliata*.

◀ *Fall*

Winter

Ribes aureum

RIBE-es O-ree-um
Golden Currant
Grossulariaceae—Currant or Gooseberry Family

Deciduous Shrub
HEIGHT: 4 to 6 feet
SPREAD: 4 to 6 feet

Illustration by
Jayme S. Irvin

*Flowers and leaves emerge at
the same time in early spring.*

Golden Currant in spring garden

Spring

Late summer

LANDSCAPE USE
Wildlife plantings, fruit gardens, low shelter-belts, background plants; ornamental use wherever an open shrubby clump is desired.

FORM
Erect, open, multi-stemmed, deciduous shrub. Forms a clump. If browsed or clipped, twigs and foliage will increase in density.

NATIVE RANGE
Inland regions of the West, Washington to Montana, south to California. Common to shadier locations in Colorado's foothills.

CHARACTERISTICS
FLOWER: spicy fragrance, showy, golden, tubular, 1-inch flowers in spring.
LEAVES: attractive, 1- to 1½-inch, bright green, maplelike leaves with red fall color.
FRUIT: edible, small, red to black currants in summer that dry on the shrub to delicious, raisin-type fruit.
BARK: smooth, gray, no spines.

CULTURE
SOIL: adaptable, but prefers well drained, sandy loam. Tolerates alkaline soil without chlorosis.
EXPOSURE: partial shade preferred. Does not tolerate dry exposed positions.
PROPAGATION: layering, cutting or sow seed in fall and mulch seed bed lightly.
WATER: low to moderate, doing best under moderate water conditions.
HARDINESS ZONES: 2 to 7. Extremely hardy, surviving well north into Canada.
LIFE SPAN: long.

BEST FEATURES
Healthy, attractive shrub spring through fall. Not bothered by wind or hail. No maintenance.

COMPANION PLANTS
For ground cover below, try Mat Penstemons, such as *Penstemon caespitosus* 'Claude Barr', *Veronica liwanensis* (Turkish Veronica) or *V. pectinata* (Woolly Veronica). Low spring bulbs, such as *Anemone blanda* would also do well under Golden Currant.

DISADVANTAGES
None.

Fall

Winter

Rubus deliciosus

ROO-bus del-liss-i-O-sus
Boulder Raspberry, Thimbleberry
Rosaceae—Rose Family

❖

Deciduous Shrub
HEIGHT: 4 to 6 feet
SPREAD: 5 to 8 feet

Illustration by
Patty Homs

Attractive spring flower and bright green leaves

*Boulder Raspberry
in summer garden*

Spring

Summer

LANDSCAPE USE
A very attractive shrub that does well in dry shade. Use in mass groupings, to attract birds and for naturalizing.

FORM
Arching branches form a loose, vase-shaped shrub.

NATIVE RANGE
Mountains and foothills of Colorado, New Mexico, Arizona, Wyoming and Oklahoma. Seen at elevations between 4,500 and 9,000 feet.

CHARACTERISTICS
FLOWER: a large, single, white roselike flower in spring and early summer.
LEAVES: bright green and lobed, yellow fall color.
FRUIT: dark purplelike raspberries. Although edible, they are not palatable. Color varies from dark purple to reddish.
STEMS: thornless, copper brown stems.

CULTURE
SOIL: prefers gravelly or silty loam, although adaptable to a variety of soil types.
EXPOSURE: sun or partial shade.
PROPAGATION: seed and cuttings.
WATER: occasional deep soaking.
HARDINESS ZONES: 4 to 8.
LIFE SPAN: long.

BEST FEATURES
Flowers are very showy, and it has an attractive form.

COMPANION PLANTS
Lamium maculatum (Spotted Dead Nettle), *Pinus ponderosa* (Ponderosa Pine), *Physocarpus monogynus* (Mountain Ninebark) and *Arctostaphylos uva-ursi* (Kinnikimick)

◀ *Fall*

Winter

173

S. *middendorfianum* ▼

S. *spectabile* ▼

▼ S. *spurium*

Illustration by
Lynn Janicki

Sedum spurium

SEE-dum SPUR-ee-um
Two-row Stonecrop
Crassulaceae—Stonecrop Family

❖

Evergreen Succulent
HEIGHT: 3 to 6 inches
SPREAD: 12 to 24 inches

LANDSCAPE USE

Colorful mat throughout the seasons, providing flower and leaf color to rock gardens, path edges and overlapping, terraced slopes.

FORM

Creeping succulent mat.

NATIVE RANGE

Northern Hemisphere, temperate and cold zones. Good to 6,500 feet in Colorado.

CHARACTERISTICS

FLOWER: star-shaped, small flowers in flat, 2-inch clusters on top of a 4- to 5-inch, upright stem. Red, yellow and white tones.
LEAVES: 1/2 inch long, soft, thick, fleshy, round, coarsely toothed, closely packed along prostrate stems, forming a loose, trailing mat. Colors may be green, bronzish or red, depending on the cultivar and the season.
FRUIT: bronze, copper, star-shaped seed head.
ROOT: shallowly along stem.

CULTURE

SOIL: tolerates low fertility levels, gravelly to heavy clay textures.
EXPOSURE: full sun to half-day shade or light, dappled shade.
TOLERATES: wind, low humidity and heat.
PROPAGATION: division or sow seed in early fall or spring. Grows fast and well from cuttings, too.
WATER: moderate water. Cannot tolerate constantly moist soil.
HARDINESS ZONES: 5 to 10.
LIFE SPAN: long; moderately fast growth.

BEST FEATURES

Particularly effective around rocks whether in a rock garden, along a path or tucked into a wall.

COMPANION PLANTS

Ephedra viridis (Green Mormon Tea) and *Sedum telephium* (Russet Showy Stonecrop).

DISADVANTAGES

Not traffic tolerant. More aggressive than other *Sedum* species, can overtake small plants in a rock garden. Not dense enough to eradicate weeds.

CULTIVARS

'Dragon's Blood'—green leaves with red edges, turning blood red in the fall; flower is bright red. 'Red Carpet'—rich red leaves and rose-red flowers. 'Tricolor'—tricolor foliage of green, cream and pink.

ILLUSTRATED SPECIES

Growing under similar conditions and a similar form to *S. spurium* is *S. middendorfianum*, a worthwhile sedum with yellow flowers in late summer on upright 6-to 12-inch tall stems. Green leaves turn red in the fall.

▲ *Dragon's Blood in early summer*

◀ *Dragon's Blood in winter*

S. middendorfianum

174

Flowerless variety

Late summer garden

Stachys lanata (S. byzantina)

STACK-iss la-NA-ta
S. byz-an-TEEN-a
Lamb's Ear
Lamiaceae—Mint Family

Herbaceous Perennial
HEIGHT: 1 to 1 ½ feet
SPREAD: 1 to 3 feet

LANDSCAPE USE
Plant as a contrast to green foliage or to set off brilliant colors in borders or perennial beds. Plant as a ground cover.

FORM
Erect flower stalks rise above low-spreading foliage rosettes.

NATIVE RANGE
Caucasus to Persia, Iran. Can be established up to 8,000 feet in Colorado

CHARACTERISTICS
FLOWER: ½-inch pinkish purple tubular flowers on 18-inch tall, thick, woolly spikes from July to frost.
LEAVES: woolly, white, 4 to 8 inches, lance-shaped in basal clumps. Velvety texture of the leaf gives the plant its common name, "Lamb's Ear."
FRUIT: small nutlets in woolly pods along flower spike.
STEM: square and woolly.

CULTURE
SOIL: dry to moist, well drained, low fertility. Particularly important to have good drainage during the winter.
EXPOSURE: sun to light shade.
PROPAGATION: seeds, cuttings and division which can be done in spring or fall.
TOLERATES: established plants tolerate heat and short periods of drought.
WATER: low. Refrain from overhead watering to prevent fungal disease.
HARDINESS ZONES: 4 to 8.
LIFE SPAN: long; divide clumps after several year's growth.

BEST FEATURES
Woolly leaves; a wonderful plant for children.

COMPANION PLANTS
Potentilla fragiformis (Strawberry Cinquefoil) and *Echinacea purpurea* (Purple Coneflower).

DISADVANTAGES
Reseeds vigorously if not deadheaded.

SUBSPECIES OR VARIETIES
S. olympica, S. byzantina 'Silver Carpet'—flowerless. Many varieties and species are available.

Illustration by
Tanya McMurtry

Leaves resemble lamb's ears.

175

Fall and winter leaf color

Summer

Symphoricarpos x chenaultii

SIM-for-i-kar-pos she-NO-e-i
Chenault Coralberry
Caprifoliaceae—Honeysuckle Family

Deciduous Shrub
HEIGHT: 3 to 4 feet
SPREAD: 3 to 6 feet

LANDSCAPE USE
Mass grouping on a steep bank; wildlife, naturalizing.

FORM
Narrow, upright, arching branches spread to the ground, creating a loose, sprawling mound.

NATIVE RANGE
Possibly a hybrid between *S. microphyllus* and *S. orbiculatus*. *S. orbiculatus* is found in the Midwest and eastern states of the United States. Good to 7,500 feet in Colorado.

CHARACTERISTICS
FLOWER: tiny, light pink, trumpetlike flowers appear in clusters in mid-spring.
LEAVES: bluish green, elliptical, small, opposite on the stem, completely covering the plant. No significant fall color change.
FRUIT: purplish to pinkish berries (drupes) with white undersides, attractive to wildlife.
BARK: brownish, very fine stems. Annual spring pruning may be necessary to remove old or damaged stems.
ROOT SYSTEM: strong and dense.

CULTURE
SOIL: adaptable to a wide range of soil types—including clay—as long as it is well drained. Tolerates alkalinity.
EXPOSURE: sun to partial shade or part-day shade.
TOLERATES: air pollution.
PROPAGATION: softwood cuttings. Remove rooted runners to plant elsewhere.
WATER: moist to dry.
HARDINESS ZONES: 4 to 10
LIFE SPAN: long.

BEST FEATURES
Attractive fruit and leaves; shade tolerant.

COMPANION PLANTS
Syringa spp. (Lilac) and *Rubus deliciosus* (Boulder Raspberry).

DISADVANTAGES
Twiggy plant, unrefined winter form; therefore, best in natural landscape.

CULTIVARS
Symphoricarpos x *chenaultii* 'Hancock' (Hancock Coralberry)—lower growing (2 feet tall).

RELATED SPECIES
S. orbiculatus (Red Coralberry)—2 to 4 feet, large, pink fruit, good yellow fall color. *S. oreophilus* (Mountain Snowberry)—2 to 4 feet, white berries, good to 10,000-foot elevation.

Graceful, arching stems are enhanced with colorful fruit in the fall.

Illustration by Tanya McMurtry

Resources

1994 Perennials Wholesale. Ft. Collins, Colorado: Gulley Greenhouse Inc., 1994.

Bailey, L. H. *The Manual of Cultivated Plants.* New York: Macmillan, 1966.

Bailey, Liberty Hyde and Ether Zoe (Revised and Expanded by the Staff of the Liberty Hyde Bailey Hortorium). *Hortus Third: A Concise Dictionary of Plants Cultivated in the United States and Canada.* New York: Macmillan Publishing Company, 1976.

Ball, Ken, et al. *Taylor's Guide to Water-Saving Gardening.* Boston: Houghton Mifflin Company, 1990.

Barr, Claude A. *Jewels of the Plains.* Minneapolis: University of Minnesota Press, 1983.

Bird, Richard. *The Complete Book of Hardy Perennials.* London: Ward Lock Limited, 1993.

Brown, Lauren. *Grasses An Identification Guide.* Boston: Houghton Mifflin Company, 1979.

Carter, Brian, Editor. *The Gardener's Palette.* New York: Doubleday, 1986.

Carter, Jack. L. *Trees and Shrubs of Colorado.* Boulder: Johnson Books, 1988.

Clausen, Ruth Rogers and Nicolas H. Ekstrom. *Perennials for American Gardens.* New York: Random House, Inc., 1989.

Coate, Barrie. *Water-Conserving Plants & Landscapes for the Bay Area.* East Bay: East Bay Municipal Utility District, 1990.

Coates, Margaret Klipstein. *Perennials for the Western Garden.* Boulder: Pruett Publishing Company, 1976.

Coombes, Allen J. *Dictionary of Plant Names.* Portland: Timber Press, 1991.

Courtenay, Booth and James H. Zimmerman. *Wildflowers and Weeds.* New York: Van Nostrand Reinhold Company, 1972.

Creasy, Rosalind. *The Complete Book of Edible Landscaping.* San Francisco: Sierra Club Books, 1982.

Davis, Bryan. *Gardener's Illustrated Encyclopedia of Trees and Shrubs.* Emmaus: Rodale Press, 1987.

Deciduous Shrubs for the Home Grounds. CSU SIA 7.415, 1988.

Denver Water Department. *Designing Your Xeriscape: Plant Focus l990.* Series 4, 1990.

DeWolf, Gordon, Ed. *Taylor's Guide to Shrubs.* Boston: Houghton Mifflin Company, 1987.

DeWolf, Gordon P. Jr., et al. *Taylor's Guide to Annuals.* Boston: Houghton Mifflin Company, 1986.

Peddie, Dick, William A., W. H. Moir and R. Spellenberg. *New Mexico Vegetation, Past, Present and Future.* Albuquerque: University of New Mexico Press, 1988.

Dirr, Michael A. *Manual of Woody Landscape Plants: Their Identification, Ornamental Characteristics, Culture, Propagation and Uses.* Champaign: Stipes Publishing Company, 1990.

Drew, John K. *Pictorial Guide to Hardy Perennials.* Kalamazoo: Merchants Publishing Company, 1984.

Dunmire, John R, et al, editors. *Sunset Western Garden Book.* Menlo Park: Lane Magazine and Book Co., 1971.

Effelson, C., T. Stephens, and D. Welsh. *Xeriscape Gardening and H_2O Conservation for the American Landscape.* New York: Macmillan, 1992.

Elias, Thomas. *Trees of North America* (Field Guide and Nat. Hist.) Book Div., Times Mirror Magazine, Inc., 1980.

Elmore, Francis H. *Shrubs and Trees of the Southwest Uplands.* Tucson: Southwest Parks and Monuments Association, 1976.

Fairchild, D. H. and J. E.- Klett. *Woody Landscape Plants for the High Plains,* Technical Bulletin LTB93-1. Fort Collins: Department of Horticulture, Colorado State University, 1993.

Feldman, Fran and Cornelia Fogle, editors. *Sunset Waterwise Gardening.* Menlo Park: Lane Publishing Co., 1989.

Ferguson, Nicole. *Right Plant, Right Place.* New York: Summit Books, 1984.

Feucht, James R. *Xeriscaping: Trees and Shrubs for Low-Water Landscapes.* CSU S IA 7.229, 1987.

Gerhold, Henry D, et al., editors. *Street Tree Factsheets.* University Park, Penn State College of Agricultural Sciences, 1993.

Green Acres Nursery, Inc. 1995 Catalog. Golden, Colorado

Harrington, H.D. *Edible Native Plants of the Rocky Mountains.* Albuquerque: University of New Mexico Press, 1967.

Harrington, H.D. *Manual of the Plants of Colorado.* Denver: Sage Books, Pub. by Alan Swallow, 1964.

Hightshoe, Gary L. *Native Trees for Urban and Rural America.* Ames: Iowa State University Foundation, 1978.

Holmes, Roger, Ed. *Taylor's Guide to Natural Gardening.* Boston: Houghton Mifflin Company, 1993.

Huxley, Anthony (Editor in Chief), Mark Griffiths (Editor), and Margot Lery (Managing Editor). *The New Royal Horticulture Society Dictionary of Gardening.* London: The Macmillan Press, Limited, 1992.

Jescavage-Bernard, Karen. "Berried in the Snow." *National Gardening,* Vol. 14, Nov./Dec., 1991, pp. 40-44.

Kelly, George W. *Shrubs for the Rocky Mountains.* Cortez: Rocky Mountain Horticultural Publishing Company, 1979.

Kelly, George W. *Trees for the Rocky Mountains.* Cortez: Rocky Mountain Horticultural Publishing Company, 1976.

Kingsbury, John M. *Poisonous Plants of United States.* Englewood Cliffs: Prentice Hall, 1964.

Knopf, Jim. *The Xeriscape Flower Gardener, Water-Wise Guide for the Rocky Mountain Region.* Boulder: Johnson Publishing Company, 1991.

Knopf, Jim. *The Waterwise Tree, Shrub & Vine Companion, A Xeriscape Guide to the Rocky Mountain Region, California and the Desert South West.* Johnson Books, Boulder, Colorado, 1998.

Knox, Gerald M. et al., editors. *Better Homes and Gardens Complete Guide to Gardening.* Des Moines: Meredith Corporation, 1980.

Lawns and Ground Covers, The Time-Life Gardener's Guide. Alexandria: Time-Life Books.

Lenhart, Frederick W. *Trees and Shrubs Identified.* Denver: Lenhart, 1980

Little Valley Wholesale Nursery 1995 Catalog. Brighton, Colorado.

Little, Elbert. *The Audubon Society Field Guide to North American Trees, Western Region*. New York: Alfred A. Knopf, 1980.

MacKenzie, David S. *Complete Manual of Perennial Ground Covers*. Englewood Cliffs: Prentice Hall, 1989.

Macoboy, Stirling. *What Flower is That?* New York: Portland Home, 1986.

Maino, Evelyn and Frances Howard. *Ornamental Trees: An Illustrated Guide to Their Selection and Care*. Berkeley: University of California Press, 19??.

McGregor, Ronald. *Flora of Great Plains*. Kansas City: Kansas University Press, 1986.

McKean, William T., Ed. *Winter Guide to Central Rocky Mountain Shrubs*. Denver: State of Colorado Department of Natural Resources Division of Wildlife, 1976.

McPhearson, Gregory and Gregory H. Graves. *Ornamental and Shade Trees for Utah: A Tree Guide for Intermountain Communities*. Logan: Cooperative Extension Service of Utah State University, ED 406, 1984.

Mish, Frederick C. et al., editors. *Merriam Webster's Collegiate Dictionary Tenth Edition*. Springfield: Merriam-Webster, Inc. , 1993.

Nelson, Ruth Ashton. *Handbook of Rocky Mountain Plants*. Estes Park: Skyland Publishers, 1979.

Nelson, Ruth Ashton. *Plants of Rocky Mountain National Park*. Estes Park: Rocky Mountain Nature Association, Inc., 1982.

Pesman, M. Walter. *Meet the Natives*. Denver Botanic Gardens: Roberts Rinehart Publishers, 1992.

Phillips, Judith. *Southwestern Landscaping with Native Plants*. Santa Fe: Museum of New Mexico Press, 1987.

Pirone, Pascal P. *Diseases and Pests of Ornamental Plants*. New York: John Wiley and Sons, Intersci. Publication, 1978.

Plant Focus Committee of Xeriscape Colorado. Xeriscape Plant Focus '88. 1988.

Plants of the Southwest 1994. Catalog, Santa Fe, New Mexico

Praeger, Lloyd R. *An Account of the Genus Sedum as Found in Cultivation*. London: Spottiswoode, Ballantyne & Co. Ltd. for the Royal Horticultural Society, 1921.

Preston, Richard J. Jr. *North American Trees*. Cambridge: The Massachusetts Institute of Technology, 1965.

Preston, Richard J. Jr. *Rocky Mountain Trees*. New York: Dover Publications, Inc., 1968.

Proctor, Rob. *Annuals: Yearly Classics for the Contemporary Garden*. New York: HarperCollins Publishers, 1991.

Rickelt, H. W. *Wild Flowers of the United States*. New York: Botanic Garden, 1973.

Robinette, G.O. *Plants, People and Environmental Quality*. USDI National Park Service, No. 2405-0479.

Rondon, Joanne. *Landscaping for Water Conservation in a Semi-arid Environment*. Aurora: City of Aurora, 1980.

Saiman, David, Meg and Bill. *A High Country Garden: Plants for the Western Garden*. Catalog. Santa Fe: A High Country Garden, 1994.

Seymour, E.L.D. *The Wise Encyclopedia*. New York: HarperCollins Publishers, 1990.

Sinclair Wayne A., et al. *Diseases of Trees and Shrubs*. Ithaca: Cornell University Press 1987.

Sinnes, A. Cort. *All About Annuals*. San Francisco: Ortho Books, Chevron Chemical Company, 1981.

Spellenberg, Richard. *The Audubon Society Field Guide to North American Wildflowers: Western Region*: Alfred A Knopf, Inc., 1979.

Springer, Lauren. *The Undaunted Garden*. Golden: Fulcrum Publishing, 1994.

Still, Steven M. *Manual of Herbaceous Plants*. Champaign: Stipes Publication Company, 1994.

Still, Steven. *Herbaceous Ornamental Plants*. Champaign: Stipes Publishing Company, 1982.

Strauch, Joseph G., Jr. and James E. Klett. *Flowering Herbaceous Perennials for the High Plains*. Fort Collins: Department of Horticulture, Colorado State University,

Sunset New Western Garden Book. Menlo Park: Lane Publishing, 1979.

Taylor's Guide to Water-Saving Plants. Boston: Houghton Mifflin Company, 1961.

Taylor, Jane. *Drought-Tolerant Plants, Waterwise Gardening for every Climate*. New York: Prentice Hall, 1993.

Taylor, Norman. *Taylor's Guide to Gardening*. Cambridge Mass.: Riverside Press, 1948.

Trees: The Yearbook of Agriculture 1949. United States Department of Agriculture. Washington: U.S. Government Printing Office, 1949.

Trelease, William. *Plant Materials of Decorative Gardening*. New York: Dover Publications, Inc., 1968.

Venning, Frank D. *Wildflowers of North America*. New York: Golden Press, 1984.

Wasowski, Sally, and Andy Wasowski, *Gardening with Native Plants of the South*, Taylor Publishing, Dallas, 1994.

Wasowski, Sally, and Andy Wasowski, *Native Gardens for Dry Climates*, Clarkson Potter, New York City, 1995.

Watson, Larry E. "Favorite Water-Wise Trees and Shrubs." *Mountain, Plain, and Garden*. The Magazine of the Denver Botanic Gardens, 1992, pp. 22-24.

Weber, William A. *Rocky Mountain Flora*. Boulder: Colorado Assoc. University Press, 1976.

Whitson, Tom D., et al., editors. *Weeds of the West*. Cheyenne: The Western Society of Weed Science, in cooperation with the Western United States Land Grant Universities Cooperative Extension Services and the University of Wyoming, 1991.

Williamson, Joseph F. (Editorial Director) and Elizabeth L. Hogan (Editor of Sunset Books). *Sunset Western Garden Book*. Menlo Park: Lane Publishing Company, 1988.

Woods, Christopher. *Encyclopedia of Perennials: A Gardener's Guide*. New York: Facts on File, 1992.

Wyman, Donald. *Trees For An American Gardens*. New York: The Macmillan Company, 1965.

Wyman, Donald. *Wyman's Garden Encyclopedia*. New York: Macmillan, 1986.

Young, James A. and Cheryl G. *Collecting, Processing and Germinating Seeds of Wildland Plants*. Portland: Timber Press, Inc., 1986.

Glossary

Achene: A small, dry, indehiscent, one-seeded fruit (as of a sunflower) developing from a simple ovary and usually having a thin pericarp attached to the seed at only one point.

Alkaline: Of, relating to, containing, or having the properties of an alkali or alkali metal: Basic; *esp, of a solution*: having a pH of more than 7.

Amendment: A material (as compost) that aids plant growth indirectly by improving the condition of the soil.

Annual: Completing the life cycle in one growing season.

Anther: The part of a stamen of a seed plant that produces and contains pollen.

Axis: A plant stem.

Basal: Arising from the base of the stem (leaves).

Biennial: Continuing or lasting for two years; specif: growing vegetatively during the first year and fruiting and dying during the second.

Bract: A leaf borne on a floral axis, especially one subtending a flower or flower cluster.

Calcareous: Growing on limestone or in soil impregnated with lime.

Calyx: The usually green or leaflike part of a flower consisting of sepals.

Catkin: A long flower cluster (as of a willow) bearing crowded flowers and prominent bracts.

Chlorosis: A diseased condition in green plants marked by yellowing or blanching.

Corymb: A flat-topped inflorescence; specif: one in which the flower stalks arise at different levels on the main axis and reach about the same height, and in which the outer flowers open first and the inflorescence is indeterminate.

Cotyledon: The first leaf or one of the first pair or whorl of leaves developed by the embryo of a seed plant or of some lower plants.

Cross-pollination: Transfer of pollen from one flower to the stigma of another.

Crown: The highest part (as of a tree).

Culm: A monocotyledonous stem (as of a grass or sedge).

Cultivar: An organism of a kind originating and persistent under cultivation.

Cutting: A piece of a plant able to grow into a new plant.

Cyme: An inflorescence in which each floral axis terminates in a single flower.

Deadhead: To remove the faded flowers of (a plant) especially to keep a neat appearance and to promote reblooming by preventing seed production.

Deciduous: Falling off or out usually at the end of a period of growth or function (leaves).

Dehisce: To discharge contents by splitting; (seed pods dehiscing at maturity).

Dioecious: Having staminate and pistallate flowers borne on different individuals.

Drupe: A partly fleshy, one-seeded fruit (as a plum or cherry) that remains closed at maturity.

Espaliere: A plant (as a fruit tree) trained to grow flat against a support.

Evergreen: Having foliage that remains green (most coniferous trees).

Exfoliate: To grow by or as if by producing or unfolding leaves.

Foliage: A mass of leaves (as of a plant or forest).

Forb: An herb other than grass.

Furrow: A marked narrow depression: Groove. A deep wrinkle.

Ground Cover: A planting of low plants (as ivy) that covers the ground in place of turf. A plant adapted for use as ground cover.

Hardy Annual: A plant with only one growing season that demonstrates vigorous good health and is capable of withstanding adverse growing conditions.

Hardscape: That part of a garden area with nothing growing, that is: rocks, walls, patios, walkways and so on.

Herbaceous: Of a stem: having little or no woody tissue and persisting usually for a single growing season.

Holdfast: A part by which a plant clings to a flat surface.

Indehiscent: Remaining closed at maturity.

Indeterminate: Characterized by sequential flowering from the lateral or basal buds to the central or uppermost buds; also: characterized by growth in which the main stem continues to elongate indefinitely without being limited by a terminal inflorescence.

Inflorescence: The manner of development and arrangement of flowers on a stem; also, a flowering stem with its appendages: a flower cluster.

Layering: To form roots where a stem comes in contact with the ground.

Leaf axil: The angle between a branch or leaf and the axis from which it arises.

Lenticel: A loose aggregation of cells that penetrates the surface (as of a stem) of a woody plant and through which gases are exchanged between the atmosphere and the underlying tissues.

Loam: A loose soil of mixed clay, sand, and silt.

Monocotyledon: Any of a class or subclass of chiefly herbaceous seed plants having an embryo with a single cotyledon, usually parallel-veined leaves, and floral organs arranged in cycles of three.

Palatable: Agreeable to the taste.

Panicle: A branched flower cluster (as of a lilac) in which each branch from the main stem has one or more flowers.

Perennial: Continuing to live from year to year.

Pergola: A structure consisting of posts supporting an open roof in the form of a treleis.

Pericarp: The ripened and variously modified walls of a plant ovary.

Petiole: A slender stem that supports a leaf.

pH: A measure of acidity and alkalinity of a solution that is a number on a scale on which a value of 7 represents neutrality and lower numbers indicate increasing acidity and higher numbers increasing alkalinity.

Pinnate: Resembling a feather especially in having similar parts arranged on opposite sides of an axis like the barbs on the rachis of a feather.

Pome: A fleshy fruit consisting of an outer, thickened, fleshy layer and a central core with usually five seeds enclosed in a capsule.

Procumbent: Being or having stems that trail along the ground without rooting.

Propagation: To reproduce or cause to reproduce biologically; to cause to spread.

Raceme: A flower cluster with flowers borne along a stem and blooming from the base toward the tip.

Renewal Pruning: To repeatedly cut off or cut back parts of a plant for a better shape or more fruitful growth.

Rhizomatous: A fleshy, rootlike, and usually horizontal, underground plant stem that forms shoots above and roots below.

Rootstock: An underground part of a plant that resembles a rhizome.

Samara: A dry, indehiscent, usually one-seeded, winged fruit (as of an ash or an elm tree); also called key.

Scarify: To cut or soften the wall of (a hard seed) to hasten germination.

Sepal: One of the modified leaves comprising a flower's calyx.

Shelterbelt: A barrier of trees and shrubs that protects (as crops) from wind and storms and lessens erosion.

Silique: A narrow, elongated, two-valved, usually many-seeded, capsule that is characteristic of the mustard family.

Stigma: A small spot, scar, or opening on a plant, usually part of the pistil of a flower that receives the pollen grains and on which they germinate.

Stolon: A horizontal branch from the base of a plant that produces new plants from buds at its tip or nodes; also called runner.

Stratify: To form or arrange in layers.

Subshrub: A perennial plant having woody stems except for the terminal part of the new growth that is killed back annually.

Succulent: Having fleshy tissues that conserve moisture (plants).

Sucker: A shoot from the roots or lower part of a plant.

Taproot: A large, main root growing straight down and giving off small side roots.

Tender Annual: A plant with only one growing season that is incapable of resisting cold or other adverse growing conditions.

Thicket: A dense growth of bushes or small trees.

Tuber: A short, fleshy, usually underground stem (as of a potato plant) bearing minute, scalelike leaves each with a bud at its base.

Umbel: An inflorescence typical of the carrot family in which the axis is very much contracted so that the stalk appears to spring from the same point to form a flat or rounded flower cluster.

Whorl: A group of parts (as leaves or petals) encircling an axis and especially a plant stem.

Printed by permission. From Merriam-Webster's Collegiate® Dictionary, Tenth Edition © 1995 by Merriam-Webster Inc.

Photographer and Illustrator Credits

PAGE: 1-2—PLANT NAME: Acer ginnala-Amur Maple; ILLUSTRATIONS: Cynthia Cano; GARDEN PHOTO: Karelle Scharff; SPRING PHOTO: Scott Stephens; SUMMER PHOTO: Ed Leland; FALL PHOTO: Ed Leland; WINTER PHOTO: Ed Leland

PAGE: 3-4—PLANT NAME: Acer sac. grandidentatum - Bigtooth Maple; ILLUSTRATIONS: Cynthia Cano; GARDEN PHOTO: Denver Water; SPRING PHOTO: Denver Water, FALL PHOTOS: Charles Mann-red, Denver Water-yellow; WINTER PHOTO: Denver Water

PAGE: 6-7—PLANT NAME: Aesculus glabra - Ohio Buckeye; ILLUSTRATIONS: Cynthia Cano; GARDEN PHOTO: Alan Rollinger; SPRING PHOTO: Scott Stephens; FALL PHOTO: Scott Stephens; WINTER PHOTO: Scott Stephens

PAGE: 8-9—PLANT NAME: Amelanchier alnifolia - Saskatoon Serviceberry; ILLUSTRATIONS: Marilyn Taylor; GARDEN PHOTO: Denver Water; SPRING PHOTO: Scott Stephens; SUMMER PHOTO: Scott Stephens; FALL PHOTO: Denver Water; WINTER PHOTO: Scott Stephens

PAGE: 10-11—PLANT NAME: Amorpha canescens - Leadplant; ILLUSTRATIONS: Marilyn Taylor; GARDEN PHOTO: Lorie Stover; SPRING PHOTO: Lorie Stover; SUMMER PHOTO: Lorie Stover; FALL PHOTO: Lorie Stover; WINTER PHOTO: Lorie Stover

PAGE: 12-13—PLANT NAME: Atriplex canescens - Four-wing Saltbush; ILLUSTRATIONS: Lori Rhea Swingle; GARDEN PHOTO: Charles Mann; SPRING PHOTO: Ed Leland; SUMMER PHOTO: Alan Rollinger; FALL PHOTO: Karelle Scharff; WINTER PHOTO: Karelle Scharff

PAGE: 14-15—PLANT NAME: Caryopteris x clandonensis - Blue Mist Spirea; ILLUSTRATIONS: Diana J. Neadeau/Zimmermann; GARDEN PHOTO: Charles Mann; SPRING PHOTO: Scott Stephens; SUMMER PHOTO: Lorie Stover; FALL PHOTO: Lorie Stover; WINTER PHOTO: Kathy Olsen

PAGE: 16-17—PLANT NAME: Catalpa speciosa - Western Catalpa; ILLUSTRATIONS: Ann Lowdermilk; GARDEN PHOTO: Scott Stephens; SPRING PHOTO: Lorie Stover; SUMMER PHOTO: Lorie Stover; FALL PHOTO: Ed Leland; WINTER PHOTO: Scott Stephens

PAGE: 18-19—PLANT NAME: Celtis occidentalis - Hackberry; ILLUSTRATIONS: Jayme Irwin; GARDEN PHOTO: Denver Water; SPRING PHOTO: Denver Water; FALL PHOTO: Scott Stephens; WINTER PHOTO: Scott Stephens

PAGE: 20-21—PLANT NAME: Ceratoides lanata - lanata - Winter Fat; ILLUSTRATIONS: Tana Pittman; GARDEN PHOTO: Alan Rollinger; SUMMER PHOTO: Robert Heapes; CLOSE-UP PHOTO: Alan Rollinger (Native Setting)

PAGE: 22-23—PLANT NAME: Cercocarpus ledifolius - Curl-leaf Mahogany; ILLUSTRATIONS: Diana J. Neadeau/Zimmermann; GARDEN PHOTO: Charles Mann; SPRING PHOTO: Denver Water; SUMMER PHOTO: Denver Water; FALL PHOTO: Denver Water; WINTER PHOTO: Denver Water

PAGE: 24-25—PLANT NAME: Chamaebatiaria millefolium - Fernbush; ILLUSTRATIONS: Susan Fisher; GARDEN PHOTO: Charles Mann; SPRING PHOTO: Ed Leland ; SUMMER PHOTO: Lorie Stover; FALL PHOTO: Ed Leland; WINTER PHOTO: Lori Stover

PAGE: 26-27—PLANT NAME: Chrysothamnus nauseosus - Rubber Rabbit Brush; ILLUSTRATIONS: Jill Sanders Buck; GARDEN PHOTO: Charles Mann; SPRING PHOTO: Ed Leland; SUMMER PHOTO: Scott Stephens; FALL PHOTO: Scott Stephens; WINTER PHOTO: Randy Tatroe

PAGE: 28-29—PLANT NAME: Cotoneaster divaricatus - Spreading Cotoneaster; ILLUSTRATIONS: Linda Lorraine Wolfe; GARDEN PHOTO: Denver Water; SPRING PHOTO: Denver Water; SUMMER PHOTO: Denver Water; FALL PHOTO: Denver Water

PAGE: 30-31—PLANT NAME: Cowania mixicana - Cliffrose; ILLUSTRATIONS: Melody Durrett; GARDEN PHOTO: Charles Mann; SUMMER PHOTOS: Alan Rollinger - seed plumes, Lorie Stover - shrub; FALL PHOTO: Lorie Stover; WINTER PHOTO: Charles Mann

PAGE: 32-33—PLANT NAME: Crataegus crus-gali - Cockspur Hawthorne; ILLUSTRATIONS: Allyn Jarrett; GARDEN PHOTO: Denver Water; SPRING PHOTO: Denver Water; SUMMER PHOTO: Denver Water; FALL PHOTO: Ken Ball; WINTER PHOTO: Denver Water

PAGE: 34-35—PLANT NAME: Fallugia paradoxa - Apache Plume; ILLUSTRATIONS: Nancy Nelson; GARDEN PHOTO: Charles Mann; SPRING PHOTO: Lorie Stover; SUMMER PHOTO: Lorie Stover; FALL PHOTO: Ed Leland; WINTER PHOTO: Lorie Stover

PAGE: 36-37—PLANT NAME: Forestiera neomexicana - New Mexico Privet; ILLUSTRATIONS: Melody Durrett; GARDEN PHOTO: Charles Mann; SPRING PHOTO: Ed Leland; FALL PHOTO: Alan Rollinger; WINTER PHOTO: Scott Stephens

PAGE: 38-39—PLANT NAME: Fraxinus pennsylvanica - Green Ash; ILLUSTRATIONS: Melody Durrett; GARDEN PHOTO: Denver Water; SPRING PHOTO: Denver Water; SUMMER PHOTO: Denver Water; WINTER PHOTO: Denver Water

PAGE: 40-41—PLANT NAME: Gymnocladus dioica - Kentucky Coffee Tree; ILLUSTRATIONS: Nancy Nelson; GARDEN PHOTO: Lorie Stover; SUMMER PHOTO: Lorie Stover; FALL PHOTO: Lorie Stover; WINTER PHOTO: Lorie Stover

PAGE: 42-43—PLANT NAME: Hippophae rhamnoides - Sea Buckthorn; ILLUSTRATIONS: Susan Fisher; GARDEN PHOTO: Alan Rollinger; SPRING PHOTO: Denver Water; FALL PHOTO: Denver Water (both); WINTER PHOTO: Ed Leland

PAGE: 44-45—PLANT NAME: Juniperus horizontalis - Creeping Juniper; ILLUSTRATIONS: Lori Rhea Swingle; GARDEN PHOTO: Ed leland 'Hughes'; SUMMER PHOTO: Ed Leland (Blue Chip), Scott Stephens (Wiltonii); WINTER PHOTO: Denver Water

PAGE: 46—PLANT NAME: Juniperus scopulorum - Rocky Mtn. Juniper; ILLUSTRATIONS: Lori Rhea Swingle; GARDEN PHOTO: Ed Leland; CLOSE-UP PHOTO: Denver Water

PAGE: 167—PLANT NAME: Cytissus scoparius 'Moonlight'; ILLUSTRATION: Pamela Hoffman; SPRING PHOTO: Charles Mann; SUMMER PHOTO: Charles Mann

PAGE: 48-49—PLANT NAME: Kolkwitzia amabilis - Beauty Bush; ILLUSTRATIONS: Rob Proctor; GARDEN PHOTO: Lorie Stover; SUMMER PHOTO: Lorie Stover; FALL PHOTO: Lorie Stover; WINTER PHOTO: Lorie Stover

PAGE 50-51—PLANT NAME: Koelreuteria paniculata - Golden Raintree; ILLUSTRATIONS: Sandie Howard; GARDEN PHOTO: Ed Leland; SUMMER PHOTO: Denver Water; FALL PHOTO: Ed Leland; WINTER PHOTO: Ed Leland

PAGE: 167—PLANT NAME: Philadephus microphyllus - Littleleaf Mock Orange; ILLUSTRATIONS: Janice Romine; GARDEN PHOTO: Alan Rollinger; SUMMER PHOTO: Charles Mann; WINTER PHOTO: Karelle Scharff

PAGE: 52—PLANT NAME: Pinus aristata - Bristlecone Pine; ILLUSTRATIONS: Marie Orlin; GARDEN PHOTO: Ed Leland; CLOSE-UP PHOTO: Robert Heapes

PAGE: 53—PLANT NAME: Pinus ponderosa - Ponderosa Pine; ILLUSTRATIONS: Marie Orlin; GARDEN PHOTO: Denver Water

PAGE: 54-55—PLANT NAME: Potentilla fruticosa - Potentilla; ILLUSTRATIONS: Ann Lowdermilk; GARDEN PHOTO: Ed Leland; SPRING PHOTO: Ed Leland; SUMMER PHOTO: Lorie Stover; FALL PHOTO: Lorie Stover; WINTER PHOTO: Lorie Stover

PAGE: 56-57—PLANT NAME: Prunus armeniaca - Apricot; ILLUSTRATIONS: Susan Fisher; GARDEN PHOTO: Charles Mann; SPRING PHOTO: Charles Mann; SUMMER PHOTO: Ed Leland; FALL PHOTO: Lorie Stover; WINTER PHOTO: Ed Leland

PAGE: 58-59—PLANT NAME: Prunus besseyi - Western Sand Cherry; ILLUSTRATIONS: Ann Lowdermilk; GARDEN PHOTO: Denver Water; SPRING PHOTO: Charles Mann; SUMMER PHOTO: Ken Ball; FALL PHOTO: Denver Water; WINTER PHOTO: Denver Water

PAGE: 60-61—PLANT NAME: Prunus virginiana - Chokecherry; ILLUSTRATIONS: Angela Overy; GARDEN PHOTO: Denver Water; SPRING PHOTO: Denver Water; SUMMER PHOTO: Denver Water; FALL PHOTO: Denver Water; WINTER PHOTO: Denver Water

PAGE: 62-63—PLANT NAME: Quercus bicolor - Swamp White Oak; ILLUSTRATIONS: Allyn Jarrett; GARDEN PHOTO: Lorie Stover; SPRING PHOTO: Lorie Stover; SUMMER PHOTO: Lorie Stover; FALL PHOTO: Lorie Stover; WINTER PHOTO: Lorie Stover

PAGE: 64-65—PLANT NAME: Quercus macrocarpa - Burr Oak; ILLUSTRATIONS: Allyn Jarrett; GARDEN PHOTO: Alan Rollinger; SPRING PHOTO: Denver Water; SUMMER PHOTO: Denver Water; FALL PHOTO: Denver Water; WINTER PHOTO: Denver Water

PAGE: 66-67—PLANT NAME: Rhus trilobata - Three Leaf Sumac; ILLUSTRATIONS: Sandie Howard; GARDEN PHOTO: Charles Mann; SPRING PHOTO: Denver Water; SUMMER PHOTO: Charles Mann; FALL PHOTO: Denver Water; WINTER PHOTO: Charles Mann

PAGE: 68-69—PLANT NAME: Rhus typhina - Staghorn Sumac; ILLUSTRATIONS: Sandie Howard; GARDEN PHOTO: Denver Water; SUMMER PHOTO: Denver Water; FALL PHOTO: Denver Water; WINTER PHOTO: Denver Water

PAGE: 70-71—PLANT NAME: Robinia neomexicana - New Mexico Locust; ILLUSTRATIONS: Marjorie C. Leggitt; GARDEN PHOTO: Karelle Scharff; SUMMER PHOTO: Denver Water; FALL PHOTO: Karelle Scharff; WINTER PHOTO: Karelle Scharff

PAGE: 72-73—PLANT NAME: Sophora japonica - Japanese Pagoda Tree; ILLUSTRATIONS: Karen Boggs; GARDEN PHOTO: Lorie Stover; SPRING PHOTO: Lorie Stover; FALL PHOTO: Lorie Stover; WINTER PHOTO: Lorie Stover

PAGE: 74-75—PLANT NAME: Spirea x vanhouttei - Vanhoutte Spirea; ILLUSTRATIONS: Linda Lorraine Wolfe; GARDEN PHOTO: Alan Rollinger; SPRING PHOTO: Charles Mann; SUMMER PHOTO: Lorie Stover; FALL PHOTO: Alan Rollinger; WINTER PHOTO: Alan Rollinger

PAGE: 76-77—PLANT NAME: Syringa vulgaris - Lilac; ILLUSTRATIONS: Linda Evans; GARDEN PHOTO: Denver Water; SPRING PHOTO: Karelle Scharff; SUMMER PHOTO: Denver Water; FALL PHOTO: Denver Water; WINTER PHOTO: Karelle Scharff

PAGE: 78-79—PLANT NAME: Viburnum lantana - Wayfaring Tree; ILLUSTRATIONS: Nancy Nelson; GARDEN PHOTO: Alan Rollinger; SPRING PHOTO: Alan Rollinger; SUMMER PHOTO: Scott Stephens; FALL PHOTO: Alan Rollinger; WINTER PHOTO: Alan Rollinger

PAGE: 80-81—PLANT NAME: Yucca species - Yucca; ILLUSTRATIONS: Susan Rubin; GARDEN PHOTO: Denver Water (glauca); SPRING PHOTO: Charles Mann (baccata); SUMMER PHOTO: Denver Water (filamentosa)

PAGE: 82—PLANT NAME: Rosa x harisonii - Harisonís Yellow Rose; ILLUSTRATIONS: Marie Orlin; GARDEN PHOTO: Charles Mann

PAGE: 84-85—PLANT NAME: Achillea species - Yarrow; ILLUSTRATIONS: Tana Pittman; SUMMER PHOTOS: Lorie Stover (Summer Pastels) & (Wooly), Charles Mann (Yarrow as Lawn), Denver Water/Karelle Scharff (Tall Yellow)

PAGE: 86—PLANT NAME: Agastache cana - Dubble Bubble Mint; ILLUSTRATIONS: Jill Buck; GARDEN PHOTO: Charles Mann

PAGE: 87—PLANT NAME: Alyssoides utriculata - Bladder Pod; ILLUSTRATIONS: Jill Buck; GARDEN PHOTO: Lorie Stover

PAGE: 88—PLANT NAME: Anacyclus depressus - Atlas Daisy; ILLUSTRATIONS: Shirley Nelson; GARDEN PHOTO: Lorie Stover; SUMMER PHOTO: Angela Overy (closed petals)

PAGE: 89—PLANT NAME: Asclepias tuberosa - Butterfly Weed; ILLUSTRATIONS: Lori Rhea Swingle; SUMMER PHOTOS: Denver Water (midsummer), Lorie Stover (late summer); FALL PHOTO: Lorie Stover

PAGE: 90—PLANT NAME: Aurinia saxatile - Basket-of-Gold; ILLUSTRATIONS: Allyn Jarrett; GARDEN PHOTO: Karelle Scharff; SPRING PHOTO: Scott Stephens; SUMMER PHOTO: Lorie Stover

PAGE: 91—PLANT NAME: Callirhoe involucrata - Wine Cup; ILLUSTRATIONS: Tanya McMurtry; SPRING PHOTO: Lorie Stover; SUMMER PHOTO: Lorie Stover

PAGE 92—PLANT NAME: Campanula rotundifolia - Bluebells; ILLUSTRATIONS: Nancy Nelson; GARDEN PHOTO: Lorie Stover; SUMMER PHOTO: Robert Heapes

PAGE: 93—PLANT NAME: Centranthus ruber - Red Valerian; ILLUSTRATIONS: Allyn Jarrett; GARDEN PHOTO: Lorie Stover

PAGE: 94-95—PLANT NAME: Campsis radicans - Trumpet Vine; ILLUSTRATIONS: Susan Rubin; GARDEN PHOTO: Ed Leland; SUMMER PHOTO: Lorie Stover; FALL PHOTO: Lorie Stover; WINTER PHOTO: Lorie Stover

PAGE: 96—PLANT NAME: Eriogonum umbellatum - Sulphur Flower; ILLUSTRATIONS: Debbie Brown Tejada; GARDEN PHOTO: Lorie Stover

PAGE: 97—PLANT NAME: Gaillardia aristata - Blanket Flower; ILLUSTRATIONS: Marie Orlin; GARDEN PHOTO: Ed Leland; FALL PHOTO: Ed Leland; WINTER PHOTO: Lorie Stover

PAGE: 98—PLANT NAME: Gutierrezia sarothrae - Snakeweed; ILLUSTRATIONS: Susan Rubin; GARDEN PHOTO: Charles Mann; SUMMER PHOTO: Charles Mann

PAGE: 99—PLANT NAME: Hemerocallis species - Daylily; ILLUSTRATIONS: Linda Lorraine Wolfe; GARDEN PHOTO: Charles Mann

PAGE 100-101—PLANT NAME: Iris hybrids - Bearded Iris; ILLUSTRATIONS: Ann Lowdermilk; GARDEN PHOTO: Denver Water; SPRING PHOTO: Lorie Stover, FALL PHOTO: Lorie Stover

PAGE: 102—PLANT NAME: Liatris Punctata; ILLUSTRATIONS: Marie Orlin; GARDEN PHOTO: Charles Mann; FALL PHOTO: Lorie Stover

PAGE: 103—PLANT NAME: Linum perenne - Blue Flax; ILLUSTRATIONS: Marjorie C. Leggitt; GARDEN PHOTO: Lorie Stover; SPRING PHOTO: Ed Leland

PAGE: 104—PLANT NAME: Nepeta X faassenii - Catmint; ILLUSTRATIONS: Cynthia Cano; GARDEN PHOTO: Charles Mann

PAGE: 105—PLANT NAME: Oenothera missouriensis - Ozark Sundrop; ILLUSTRATIONS: Karen Boggs; GARDEN PHOTO: Charles Mann; SUMMER PHOTO: Lorie Stover

PAGE: 106—PLANT NAME: Parthenocissus quinquefolia - Virginia Creeper; ILLUSTRATIONS: Linda Evans; SUMMER PHOTO: Denver Water; FALL PHOTO: Denver Water

PAGE: 107—PLANT NAME: Perovskia atriplicifolia - Russian Sage; ILLUSTRATIONS: Tanya Pittman; GARDEN PHOTO: Ed Leland; SUMMER PHOTO: Denver Water; WINTER PHOTO: Scott Stephens

PAGE: 108-109—PLANT NAME: Penstemon species; ILLUSTRATIONS: Angela Overy; GARDEN PHOTO: Denver Water (Sunset P.); SPRING PHOTO: Robert Heapes (MAT. P.); SUMMER PHOTOS: Charles Mann (Sand P.), (Scarlet Bugler), Robert Heapes (Slender P.)

PAGE: 110—PLANT NAME: Polygonum aubertii - Silver Lace Vine; ILLUSTRATIONS: Cynthia Cano; SUMMER PHOTO: Scott Stephens; WINTER PHOTO: Denver Water

PAGE: 111—PLANT NAME: Pulsatilla vulgaris - European Pasqueflower; ILLUSTRATIONS: Linda Evans; GARDEN PHOTO: Lorie Stover, SPRING PHOTO: Charles Mann; SUMMER PHOTO: Lorie Stover

PAGE: 112—PLANT NAME: Ratibida columnifera - Prairie Coneflower; ILLUSTRATIONS: Angela Overy; GARDEN PHOTO: Lorie Stover

PAGE: 113—PLANT NAME: Salvia officinalis - Garden Sage; ILLUSTRATIONS: Debbie Brown Tejada; GARDEN PHOTO: Charles Mann

PAGE: 114—PLANT NAME: Stanleya pinnata - Prince's Plume; ILLUSTRATIONS: Jill Buck; SUMMER PHOTO: Charles Mann

PAGE: 115—PLANT NAME: Tanacetum densum - Partridge feather; ILLUSTRATIONS: Susan Rubin; GARDEN PHOTO: Alan Rollinger; SUMMER PHOTO: Charles Mann

PAGE: 116—PLANT NAME: Zauschneria arizonica Arizona Zauschneria; ILLUSTRATIONS: Sandie Howard; GARDEN PHOTO: Lorie Stover

PAGE: 118—PLANT NAME: Turf - Agropyron cristatum - Crested Wheat Grass; ILLUSTRATIONS: none; GARDEN PHOTO: Lorie Stover

PAGE: 119—PLANT NAME: Antennaria rosea - Pink Pussytoes; ILLUSTRATIONS: Susan Rubin; GARDEN PHOTO: Lorie Stover; SUMMER PHOTO: Alan Rollinger; CLOSE-UP PHOTO: Lorie Stover

PAGE: 120—PLANT NAME: Bouteloua curtipendula - Sideoats Gramma; ILLUSTRATIONS: Debbie Brown Tejada; GARDEN PHOTO: Charles Mann; SUMMER PHOTO: Lorie Stover

PAGE: 121—PLANT NAME: Turf - Bouteloua gracilis - Blue Gramma; ILLUSTRATIONS: Beckie Smith (mower); GARDEN PHOTO: Denver Water

PAGE: 122—PLANT NAME: Turf - Buchloe dactyloides - Buffalograss; ILLUSTRATIONS: none; GARDEN PHOTO: Denver Water

PAGE: 123—PLANT NAME: Calamagrostis acutiflora - Karl Foerster FRG; ILLUSTRATIONS: Nancy Nelson; GARDEN PHOTO: Denver Water; WINTER PHOTO: Scott Stephens

PAGE: 124—PLANT NAME: Cerastium tomentosum - Snow-in Summer; ILLUSTRATIONS: Tanya McMurtry; GARDEN PHOTO: Denver Water; FALL PHOTO: Scott Stephens

PAGE: 125—PLANT NAME: Delosperma cooperii - Pink Hardy Ice Plant; ILLUSTRATIONS: Angela Overy; GARDEN PHOTO: Denver Water; SUMMER PHOTO: Denver Water; WINTER PHOTO: Denver Water

PAGE: 126—PLANT NAME: Delosperma nubigenum - Hardy Yellow Ice Plant; ILLUSTRATIONS: Angela Overy; GARDEN PHOTO: Robert Heapes; SUMMER PHOTO: Scott Stephens; WINTER PHOTO: Robert Heapes

PAGE: 127—PLANT NAME: Turf - Festuca arundinacea - Tall Fescue; ILLUSTRATIONS: Beckie Smith (mower); GARDEN PHOTO: Lorie Stover

PAGE: 128—PLANT NAME: Festuca Ovina Glauca - Blue Fescue; ILLUSTRATIONS: Sandie Howard; GARDEN PHOTO: Charles Mann

PAGE: 129—PLANT NAME: Helictotrichon sempervirens - Blue Avena Grass; ILLUSTRATIONS: Diana J. Neadeau/Zimmermann; GARDEN PHOTO: Denver Water; FALL PHOTO: Charles Mann

PAGE 130-131—PLANT NAME: Miscanthus sinensis - Miscanthus Grass; ILLUSTRATIONS: Pamela Hoffman; GARDEN PHOTO: Connie Ellifson; SUMMER PHOTO: Denver Water; FALL PHOTO: Denver Water; WINTER PHOTO: Denver Water

PAGE: 132—PLANT NAME: Oryzopsis hymenoides - Indian Rice Grass; ILLUSTRATIONS: Susan T. Fisher; GARDEN PHOTO: Charles Mann

PAGE: 133—PLANT NAME: Pennisetum alopecuroides - Fountain Grass; ILLUSTRATIONS: Debbie Brown Tejada; GARDEN PHOTO: Charles Mann; WINTER PHOTO: Denver Water

PAGE: 134—PLANT NAME: Pennisetum setaceum 'Rubrum' - Purple Fountain Grass; ILLUSTRATIONS: Debbie Brown Tejada; GARDEN PHOTO: Denver Water

PAGE: 135—PLANT NAME: Santolina chamaecyparissus - Lavender Cotton; ILLUSTRATIONS: Melody Durrett; GARDEN PHOTO: Connie Ellifson; FALL PHOTO: Karelle Scharff

PAGE: 136-137—PLANT NAME: Polygonum affine - Himalayan Fleeceflower; ILLUSTRATIONS: Sandie Howard; GARDEN PHOTO: Denver Water; SPRING PHOTO: Scott Stephens; SUMMER PHOTO: Denver Water; FALL PHOTO: Alan Rollinger; WINTER PHOTO: Denver Water

PAGE: 138—PLANT NAME: Sedum spectabile - Showy Stonecrop; ILLUSTRATIONS: Lynn Janicki; SPRING PHOTO: Lorie Stover; SUMMER PHOTO: Ed Leland; FALL PHOTO: Denver Water/Karelle Scharff

PAGE: 139—PLANT NAME: Sempervivum species-Hens and Chicks; ILLUSTRATIONS: Susan Rubin; GARDEN PHOTO: Lorie Stover; SPRING PHOTO: Lorie Stover; SUMMER PHOTO: Lorie Stover

PAGE: 140—PLANT NAME: Thymus pseudolanuginosus - Wooll Thyme; ILLUSTRATIONS: Marilyn Taylor; SUMMER PHOTO: Robert Heapes; WINTER PHOTO: Scott Stephens

PAGE: 141—PLANT NAME: Veronica pectinata - Blue Woolly Speedwell; ILLUSTRATIONS: Susan Rubin; GARDEN PHOTO: Angela Overy, SPRING PHOTO: Lorie Stover; SUMMER PHOTO: Lorie Stover

PAGE: 142—PLANT NAME: Zinnia grandiflora - Desert Zinnia; ILLUSTRATIONS: Marilyn Taylor; GARDEN PHOTO: Denver Water; SUMMER PHOTO: Charles Mann

PAGE: 144—PLANT NAME: Coreopsis tinctoria - Tickseed; ILLUSTRATIONS: Ann Lowdermilk; GARDEN PHOTO: Lorie Stover

PAGE: 145—PLANT NAME: Cosmos bipinnatus - Cosmos; ILLUSTRATIONS: Karen Boggs; GARDEN PHOTO: Denver Water/Karelle Scharff; SUMMER PHOTO: Lorie Stover

PAGE: 146—PLANT NAME: Eschscholzia californica - California Poppy; ILLUSTRATIONS: Tanya McMurtry, SUMMER PHOTO: Ed Leland

PAGE: 147—PLANT NAME: Gomphrena globosa - Globe Amaranth; ILLUSTRATIONS: Tana Pittman; GARDEN PHOTO: Rob Proctor

PAGE: 148—PLANT NAME: Lavatera trimestris - Annual Mallow; ILLUSTRATIONS: Linda Evans; GARDEN PHOTO: Rob Proctor; CLOSE-UP PHOTO: Rob Proctor

PAGE: 149—PLANT NAME: Portulaca grandiflora - Moss Rose; ILLUSTRATIONS: Karen Boggs; SUMMER PHOTO: Scott Stephens

PAGE: 150—PLANT NAME: Salvia sclarea - Clary Sage; ILLUSTRATIONS: Debbie Brown Tejada; GARDEN PHOTO: Denver Water

PAGE: 151—PLANT NAME: Sanvitalia procumbens - Creeping Zinnia; ILLUSTRATIONS: Ann Lowdermilk; GARDEN PHOTO: Lorie Stover; CLOSE-UP PHOTO: Lorie Stover

PAGE: 152—PLANT NAME: Tropaeolum majus - Nasturtium; ILLUSTRATIONS: Lori Rhea Swingle; WINTER PHOTO: Robert Heapes

PAGE: 153—PLANT NAME: Zinnia angustifolia - Narrow Leaf Zinnia; ILLUSTRATIONS: Angela Overy; GARDEN PHOTO: Rob Proctor

PAGE: 156—PLANT NAME: Alchemilla mollis - Ladies Mantle; ILLUSTRATIONS: Susan Rubin; GARDEN PHOTO: Lorie Stover

PAGE: 157—PLANT NAME: Arctostaphylos uva-ursi - Kinnikinnick; ILLUSTRATIONS: Nancy Nelson; SPRING PHOTO: Lorie Stover

PAGE: 158—PLANT NAME: Bergenia cordifolia - Heartleaf Bergenia; ILLUSTRATIONS: Harriet Olds; GARDEN PHOTO: Panayoti Kelaidis

PAGE: 159—PLANT NAME: Brunnera macrophylla - Perennial Forget-Me-Not; ILLUSTRATIONS: Nancy Nelson; SPRING PHOTO: Lorie Stover

PAGE: 160—PLANT NAME: Calamintha grandiflora - Beautiful Mint; ILLUSTRATIONS: Jayme S. Irvin; SUMMER PHOTO: Lorie Stover

PAGE: 161—PLANT NAME: Campanula portenschlagiana - Dalmation Bellflower; ILLUSTRATIONS: Cynthia Cano; GARDEN PHOTO: Lorie Stover

PAGE: 162—PLANT NAME: Galium odoratum - Sweet Woodruff; ILLUSTRATIONS: Marilyn Taylor; SPRING PHOTO: Lorie Stover

PAGE: 163—PLANT NAME: Heuchera sanguinea - Corallbells; ILLUSTRATIONS: Linda Lorraine Wolfe; GARDEN PHOTO: Denver Water (shade); SPRING PHOTO: Lorie Stover (sun)

PAGE: 164—PLANT NAME: Lamium maculatum - Spotted Dead Nettle; ILLUSTRATIONS: Libby Kyer; SPRING PHOTO: Lorie Stover

PAGE: 165—PLANT NAME: Mahonia repens - Creeping Grapeholly; ILLUSTRATIONS: Jill Buck; GARDEN PHOTO: Denver Water; SPRING PHOTO: Denver Water; SUMMER PHOTO: Scott Stephens; WINTER PHOTO: Denver Water

PAGE: 167—PLANT NAME: Rosa glauca - Redleaf Rose; ILLUSTRATIONS: Linda Evans; GARDEN PHOTO: Lorie Stover

PAGE: 168-169—PLANT NAME: Ptelea trifoliata - Wafer Ash; ILLUSTRATIONS: Susan Rubin; GARDEN PHOTO: Alan Rollinger; SUMMER PHOTO: Alan Rollinger; FALL PHOTO: Charles Mann; WINTER PHOTO: Alan Rollinger; CLOSE-UP PHOTO: Alan Rollinger

PAGE: 170—PLANT NAME: Ribes aureum - Golden Currant; ILLUSTRATIONS: Jayme S. Irvin; GARDEN PHOTO: Alan Rollinger; SPRING PHOTO: Ed Leland; SUMMER PHOTO: Denver Water; FALL PHOTO: Denver Water; WINTER PHOTO: Kathy Olsen

PAGE: 172-173—PLANT NAME: Rubus deliciosus - Thimbleberry; ILLUSTRATIONS: Patty Homs; GARDEN PHOTO: Alan Rollinger; SPRING PHOTO: Lorie Stover; SUMMER PHOTO: Lorie Stover; FALL PHOTO: Scott Stephens; WINTER PHOTO: Lorie Stover

PAGE: 174—PLANT NAME: Sedum spurium - Two-row Stonecrop & S. middendorffanum; ILLUSTRATION: Lynn Janicki; SPRING PHOTO: Charles Mann; SUMMER PHOTO: Ed Leland; WINTER PHOTO: Angela Overy -(S. middendorffanum)

PAGE: 175—PLANT NAME: Stachys lanata - Lambis Ear; ILLUSTRATIONS: Tanya McMurtry; GARDEN PHOTO: Lorie Stover; SUMMER PHOTO: Charles Mann

PAGE: 176—PLANT NAME: Symphoricarpos X Chenaultii -Hancock Coralberry; ILLUSTRATIONS: Tanya McMurtry; SUMMER PHOTO: Denver Water; FALL PHOTO: Denver Water

Index